DEEP WILD
Writing from the Backcountry

"The most alive is the wildest."
Henry David Thoreau

VOLUME 4 - 2022

Deep Wild Journal is published once a year in the summer.

Subscriptions are $20 for one year, $35 for two and $45 for three, postage paid anywhere in the United States. Student rates are $14/year. Contact us for international rates. Selected back issues are also available at discounted rates. Please see *deepwildjournal.com/subscribe* or email us at *deepwildorders@gmail.com*.

Submissions are open in the fall for the following year's issue. Please see *deepwildjournal.com/submit* for details on how, when, and where to submit your work.

Community: To stay in touch, follow us on Facebook, Twitter, or Instagram, or on our blog at *deepwildjournal.com/blog*. Correspondences should be addressed to the appropriate editor and sent to *deepwildjournal@gmail.com*.

This volume was printed on FSC (Forest Stewardship Council)-certified paper by All-American Printing, Petaluma, California.
ISBN: 978-1-7372874-2-1

Cover Art by Bessann Swanson
Used with permission.
Front: "Halls Creek Cottonwood" Back: "Canyoneer"
Watercolor on paper
Utah Canyonlands

Interior Art by Andie Thrams
© 2022. Used with permission.
Whiskey, Tango, Foxtrot
Hectograph, ink, watercolor, gouache, and tree resin on kozo.
9 x 9 inches

DEEP WILD
Writing from the Backcountry

Founder and Nonfiction Editor............ Rick Kempa
Poetry Editor.............................Heidi Blankenship
Fiction Editor...................................Janet Goldberg
Assistant Editor .... Corrinne Brumby
Graphic Designer.............................Dave Gutierrez
Distribution Manager..................... Fern Stringham
Technical Consultant.................... Bradley McGinty
Advertising Specialist...................... Aaron Denham

The mission of *Deep Wild: Writing from the Backcountry*
is to publish the best work we can find in celebration of,
and in defense of, places where there are no roads.

Contents

Artist Andie Thrams at work amidst the redwoods.
Photo by Dennis Eagan

Foreword

There is peace to be found in *Deep Wild 2022*, of the soul-satisfying sort we crave. Bessann Swanson's watercolor cover image, "Halls Creek Cottonwood," emanates it. Susan McMillan and companion, their "canoe adrift / like a stick on rambling current in idle autumn breeze," are mesmerized by the loon that "trails long ribbons of gold over the lake's dark face." Christopher Norment, in his *haibun* "Narrow Trail to the Western Pass," recites for us the litany of the wildflowers he encounters on his solitary walk: "phlox, lupine, spring beauty, stonecrop, several species of buckwheat, paintbrush, larkspur in wet places, on and on."

And, lest our pulses grow too slow, there is adventure: Steve Gardiner hacking at the snow on the flank of Mt. Rainier with his ice axe to "get inside the mountain" and survive a blizzard; Kelsey Wellington, our Graduate Student Essay Contest winner, hobbling for miles through deep powder with a torn ACL to get to the trailhead; Talley Kayser and her band of "ragtag scruffy bipeds" sleeping in the desert dirt at night, climbing fractured piles of rock by day, as free as they will ever be.

Unease pervades these pages as well. "Asters / shake their furled fists" and "the bare upper limbs / of the scrub oak / scratch the cloudless sky" in Cadence Summers' short poems. Swollen creeks interpose themselves between our goals and us. "The wind has shed its empathy," Eric le Fatte writes. It shreds the Lakota trail flags on Black Elk Peak in Nicholas Trandahl's poem, and all but blows Diane Gansauer and her party off the side of a mountain. The couple in Frank Haberle's story "Zone 28," clinging together in their tiny tent on an exposed ridge in Denali, are helpless before its fury.

The turbulence is within us too. We take our fears to the backcountry, seeking strength, and our grief for lost loved ones, hoping for release. "In this leafless woodland," Irish poet Maeve McKenna writes, "I have come / to walk into my father's death." Emmy Savage, alone in the high country, contemplates "the difference between cold and warmth, darkness and light, menace and joy." The fears are not unfounded: Bret Serbin and her partner, in "Out in the Backcountry," unnerved by recent violence inflicted upon gay women in campgrounds, beat a panicky retreat until they are "back on pavement, where we let ourselves believe we were safe."

These feelings are not just for ourselves but for our planet and the creatures with whom we share it. Marc Beaudin in "25 Bears" fears for the few remaining grizzly on the Yaak River "living / their perfect ursine lives," and for our children, who must live in the diminished world we bequeath them. The creatures depicted in Andie Thrams' artwork interspersed throughout this volume haunt us with their vulnerability. "What if I can't get home?" says a bat, suspended in flight against a fire-lit night sky. Roxanne, the character in Dian Parker's story "Our One and Only," is so tormented by the onslaught of bad news about the world that she—and we with her—are overwhelmed.

And yet the caribou still make their long trek south and north and south, as Dick Anderson testifies. The geese returning to the pond in November once again take Wally Swist's breath away. "What it is to see them again," he exclaims, "what it is / ...for them to have flown and then landed." Sarah Scruggs, in "Between Trees," takes her "hopelessness... blame...regret...hurt" into the backcountry and finds comfort there in the stars that "never left," strength in the "grasses rustling with the wind," a "renewed mindset" for the new day. For Roxanne in Parker's story, the despair of daylight yields to her cultivation of a skill we will all need if we are to survive the Anthropocene: dreaming together the same dream of action and renewal, willing it into reality.

"When will we awaken to all that connects us?" Andie Thrams asks, in her image of the interwoven stems and leaflets and roots on the forest floor. And in another of her images: "What if we all acted in unison?"

Laura Girardeau and her fellow "hooters," an impassioned, courageous tribe, give us one stirring answer, as they "fly through the forest" in pursuit of the spotted owl they have glimpsed in the treetops, trailing him home so that they can protect the nest and the square mile of old growth forest that surrounds it. "Who will speak for the trees?" Thrams asks. They do.

Nature rewards us for the attention we give it, as Peter Anderson affirms in "The Wheel," with evidence of resilience. The unbroken cycle of the swallows and nighthawks and bats and bluebirds, of the bear and the elk, the columbines and bee plants and black-eyed Susans, of the yellow aspen leaves and snow-white ptarmigans and spring green cottonwood and many-hued meadow—of every plant, every creature his keen eye observes, "offers some hope, even in this precarious era, that what has been will be again."

It takes a village to make a lit mag, as we have discovered in the past four years. Thanks are always in order, and we tender ours to the 51 writers and two artists who enliven these pages, as well as to the several hundred others who entrusted us with their work. We are sorry we did not have room to publish more. The "we," for whom I have special gratitude, are Poetry Editor Heidi Blankenship and Graphic Designer Dave Gutierrrez, who have invested their energies and skills in *Deep Wild Journal* from Day One, and two new additions to the team: Fiction Editor Janet Goldberg, who nurtured six excellent stories into print, and Corrinne Brumby, for whom the title Assistant Editor came to mean a dozen different things. Special thanks also to Alaskan writer Marybeth Holleman, who, along with Corrinne, served as judge for the Graduate Student Essay Contest. And finally, gratitude to you, reader, who by the fact that you hold this book in hand demonstrate your love for wild places and good words. Your interest and support mean everything to us.

Rick Kempa

© 2022 by Andie Thrams

Simple Pleasures

Charles Finn

I would like to live at the pace of stones
Have a mountain's idea of time
Spend my days in the company of shadows
Companion to inchworm, turtle, and tree.

It's hard, wouldn't you agree? Everything happening so fast
And knowing so little, only that life must end
Yet here we are—you, me, every last one of us—
Forever and always just getting started.

Which is why I come down to the river
Simple pleasures, that's what it tells me
A kingfisher spiking into the water, a cottonwood leaning in
Trout asleep in the shadows. I close my eyes

Let my mind drift downstream, breathe.

Mountain Water

Susan Marsh

Springing milky-sweet
From the glacier's hem
A slap of newborn water
Clear and bold as single-malt
At 37 degrees, with notes
Of lichen, dolomite, and moss.
It numbs the tongue.

Against its chill
Teeth tighten in their sockets.
This water is a sacrament
A concentrate of geologic time
Of gravity and friction
Slowly carving a gorge
Into the mountain. Stand

In its fine spray, bear witness
To the birth of a great river.
Lean into a mica-bright pool,
Cup both hands, lift, and drink.
Slurp without grace or shame
Greedily, hungrily, gratefully
Lips locking fishlike in your palm.

You would climb all day for this moment.

Hanging with Whales

Lorraine Hanlon Comanor

Three miles off the coast of Moorea, close to where the divemaster recently spotted spouts, I slip hesitantly over the side of the tender into the vast blue. Just up from our morning dive with some three hundred blacktip reef sharks, I'm not wildly enthusiastic about an imminent swim with whales, but I snorkel up, as everyone else is going.

Humpbacks are gentle, even helpful creatures, the guide assures me, suitable for visiting during their rest periods. If you find one on the ocean floor, you can hang out above it and it will avoid you, using its sonar when it breaches. Supposedly.

A leap of faith for someone cognizant that humpbacks range from 39 to 52 feet in length and weigh some 66,000 pounds (36 metric tons). A slight miscalculation on their part could have an undesirable outcome. Cautiously, I start finning in the opposite direction of my companions, not wanting an audience if I decide to retreat.

I score on the low end of what psychologists call the thrill-seeking spectrum. Had I scored further up the curve, I would have been more daring on the ice in my figure skating days, jumping higher, faring better. Preferring to sit under a tree with a book, I've had to goad myself to learn to fly an airplane and to dive in the deep. I envy the bold, which leads me sometimes to test my courage by doing things like swimming with sharks and hanging with whales.

In the still, clear water, I paddle several hundred yards, focused on the sandy bottom, before spying a large mass fitting the description of a resting whale. As instructed, I float face down some six feet behind what appears to be the head. Expecting up to a thirty-minute wait before this giant breaches, an estimated hundred yards ahead, I breathe slowly through my snorkel, questioning if I will have the courage to stay put when he makes his move.

After about ten minutes, I sense another presence. Just beneath the water's surface to my left is a knobby, pointy thing, dark on top, cream-colored underneath. Although underwater objects appear 33% bigger and 25% closer than they actually are, whatever this thing is, it's very large and very close. I study it for a few seconds and then look ahead, wondering if it's attached to anything. That's when I see the football-sized eye and realize that, even taking underwater distortion into account, I'm just a few feet off the end of a humpback flipper—at sixteen feet, the largest appendage in the world. It seems our divemaster failed to mention that humpbacks also rest on the surface. I look forward again to the eye, which, even if it's only the size of cow's, might as well belong to God.

For a few seconds, a mote of a human and a giant Leviathan lock gazes, each taking the other into account. Momentarily, I forget that we are too close, that if he decides to slap that flipper, I'm a goner. The sensation of being scrutinized by an intellect comparable to a human's and belonging to such an enormous creature drains whatever cognitive reserves I have left. As he continues to hold me in his gaze, I come to imagine him asking why I am doubting my courage, before realizing courage is not the issue here, as, for me, courage is defined by action in the face of vulnerability, and I am doing nothing aside from holding still. I continue to exist only by his goodwill. For how many seconds we silently communicate, I'm unsure. "Time is a puzzling thing," Thomas Mann informs us, with nothing "to mark its passage." Eventually, I tell myself to breathe, as resting whales must remind themselves to breathe, before gently backing up, reluctantly breaking our contact and relinquishing my breach-viewing spot. He moves slowly forward, and after a few moments I turn towards the tender, knowing I've traded a test of courage for a once-in-a-lifetime moment of grace.

November, Migration

Wally Swist

We hear them barking beyond
    the tall crowns of tulip trees above
our heads, as they emerge from
    the edges of the fluttering russet
leaves, the large flock of them,
    exhausted, hoarsely calling, one
after another slowing their flight,
    then circling as a group, an avian
choreography, which brings them
    closer to their reflections moving
along the surface of the pond. How
    they lift their wings, concomitantly,
to lower themselves into
    the water, to drift in free fall, each
one splashing and dragging
    its body into the churning spray
they create, each one a susurration
    punctuating the conclusion of its
flight, with a hiss, and their
    mingling honking cries, until they
rest and bob in the waves they
    launched, one by one, and as a flock,
rippling along the shore, enrapt
    in a moment of silence, which washes
over them and ourselves, filling us.
    What it is to see them again, what it is,
with such subtle astonishments,
    for them to have flown and then landed.

What's the Bear's Name?

Eric Aldrich

The game warden pulled into the worn camping area at Deer Creek trailhead about an hour and a half after Axl and I got there. The warden's white truck hauled a trailer containing a quad and a mule that he unloaded into a campsite and a corral. It was late afternoon in early June, still over 90 degrees. Heat reflected in the dry, tan grass that carpeted everything to the mountainous edge of the Arizona sky. The gray-headed peaks of the Galiuro Mountains loomed closest, our destination.

Axl and I were headed into the remote mountain range to visit Power's Mine, the site of a historic shootout and starting point for the biggest manhunt in Arizona history. In 1918, the sheriff's posse tried to apprehend the draft-dodging Power brothers and things turned ugly. Despite the Power homestead's dark history and its location far into the backcountry of Coronado National Forest, some cabins remain, maintained by volunteers.

Within the time between our arrival and when the warden joined us, Axl consumed half a bag of psylocibin mushrooms. He offered some (he's not stingy), but I declined, considering our lack of cell signal, the fact that I drove, and the miles back to paved roads. Shaded by a large oak on an early summer afternoon, I felt more satisfied with reality than usual anyway.

"Where you boys headed?" The warden asked as he approached. Cowboy hat, mustache, metal-framed sunglasses with amber lenses. I sat on the open tailgate of my truck and Axl stood awkwardly aside and behind the warden. He held his head angularly toward the conversation, a broad hat cocked over a bandana and sunglasses not unlike the warden's. I wondered what Axl's brain was doing.

"We're going out to Power's Cabin," I told the warden. He looked at me, glanced over his shoulder at Axl.

"Might not find water," the warden offered. "Even at Power's Spring."

"Right on," I kept talking, grateful for my choice to abstain from the mushrooms. "We're lugging a lot."

"You boys from Phoenix?" the warden asked a forensic question.

"Yeah," I said.

"Be careful when you get into Rattlesnake Canyon," he pointed toward the hills. "There's a bear there you'll want to look out for."

Suddenly, Axl loudly and clearly inquired: "What's the bear's name?"

The warden's eyebrows went up and his head swiveled toward my partner.

"What canyon?" I corrected, falsely. "What canyon did you say the bear's in?"

The warden's head came back my way. "Rattlesnake Canyon..."

"Oh yeah, I definitely remember that from the map," I nodded. "We'll be careful."

"You got a gun or bear spray?" He asked.

"Sure do," I lied.

When I later asked Axl what he was thinking, he broke into laughter and prevaricated. After the mushrooms wore off, he seemed too embarrassed to explain. When I brought it up again a couple of months later, he'd apparently forgotten asking the question.

I remember his question, though, because over time I've come to ask something broader: Why shouldn't a bear have a name? Why can't we respect bears as unique individuals without projecting humanity onto them? When people believe everyone in a particular population to be the same, that misunderstanding results in prejudice, fear, and violence. Does the same not hold true if we deny individualism to bears?

It's also worth pointing out that, unlike English, some Native American languages divide the world into living/nonliving rather than human/nonhuman. In "Learning the Language of Animacy," Robin Wall Kimmerer observes, "In English, we never refer to a member of our family, or indeed to any person, as *it*. That would be a profound act of disrespect. It robs a person of selfhood and kinship, reducing a person to a mere thing. So it is that in Potawatomi and most other Indigenous languages, we use the same words to address the living world as we use for our family. Because they are our family." There's no evidence that the living/nonliving construction in Indigenous languages has resulted in rampant anthropomorphizing, or harm to humans or animals. On the contrary, linguistically reducing much of the living world to mere things has caused abundant harm.

Of course, even English speakers routinely use human pronouns for animals, i.e., "How's your dog?" "He's good." The first question dog owners often get asked is, "What's your dog's name?" Affording individuality to dogs and other pet animals has created a whole system of animal welfare laws. Why shouldn't wild black bears be given the same sort of species-appropriate consideration?

If the bear's name was Erwin and we knew Erwin had been living in Rattlesnake Canyon for a number of years, maybe our respect for the bear's space and right to be there would mirror how we respect those rights for humans. Were a wildlife biologist to observe Erwin, the bear would exhibit patterns and combinations of behaviors unique from others of the species Ursus americanus. Erwin is not just "a bear," but a particular black bear.

Hikers should never expect Erwin to meet any human standards of behavior or motivation, but understanding a black bear's needs shared in common with humans—security, privacy, relaxation and so on—may help foster respect, bear by bear. More and more, humans expand into bear habitat and disrupt their food resources. What do bears do? Adapt. They live on our margins and take advantage of our waste. Attacks are rare. Black bears are learning to live where we live and to accommodate our behaviors. When we venture into the backcountry, people should learn how the bears live and accommodate the bears' behaviors. Don't leave trash, watch your dogs, keep the noise down but don't sneak around. It's common courtesy anywhere, really.

I think Axl should be free to inquire about the bear's name, and perhaps, if the bear is unnamed, he could even assign an honorary title, such as Erwin. The bear would have no idea he was Erwin, but the freedom to encounter living plants and animals as persons would remind a human of their place in nature, not as alien overlords visiting an unforgiving wilderness, but as fellow animals.

25 Bears

Marc Beaudin

The promise of flycatchers
hidden in the deep wood
tease of song from the shadows

The diamond light of water
breaking into river's breath
against the faces of rock

The caress of cedared wind
& undulations of fir trees
standing-room-only on a west-facing slope

The scant clouds pawing their way
across the sky-blue sky
that is nothing but sky-blue

The taste of this coffee
on the cabin's deck high above
the voicings of the Yaak River

& all the rest of it
made richer by the fact of those
remaining 25 grizzlies

somewhere
out there living
their perfect ursine lives

Without them, colors fade to sepia
sounds to a distant tin & we lose
some part of ourselves impossible

to describe to future generations
who will grow old believing
that the natural shape of their soul

is to have a cold dark nothing
lodged at its center—a hole the size
of a bear track in the spring mud

© 2022 by Andie Thrams

Falling Stars, City Lights, Juniper

Jay Paine

Falling Stars

The woman longed to see a falling star. The woman longed even more to see a falling star that would grant her a wish, so every night she would sit on the steep slope hoping one might fall like one of those bitter berries ripened between the flat needles of the young junipers surrounding her. Then it happened: The Milky Way's wound reopened, and hundreds of stars leaked into the sky like silvery blood droplets. Drenched in the starlight, the woman hurriedly wished to see the Milky Way heal, and the falling stars granted her wish. When the starlight lifted, her body stiffened into a thick trunk and her arms extended into long branches with whorls of flat needles spreading beneath the stars. For over a millennium, she would stand there watching the slow scabbing of the wound, the white light clotting around dark scar tissue.

City Lights

No one intends to harm the night sky, but so many contribute to its slow death by erecting street lamps on every corner and letting the taller buildings scatter light upward, infecting the wound. Though no longer visible, the Milky Way suffers, and the juniper mourns, sap beading on her bark like teardrops.

Juniper

I hiked five miles to rest my hand on this old juniper who has stood here for over 1500 years, the circumference of her white-weathered trunk measuring just over twenty-three feet. Canyon winds have sanded her bark into a gray dust where only the soft etch of bark remains like an ancient thumbprint. I let my fingers catch in the split gaps of her wood before I take a step back to admire her corkscrewed limb with a brittle branch pointing toward the sky like an arthritic finger. I can't tell what she's pointing at, but I examine the twig harboring her last whorl of green needles. She is almost dead. I study the sign saluting her scientific classification: *J. Scopulorum* of the Cypress family, and I want to ask her: *What is it that I'm supposed to mourn?*

Retrieval

Leath Tonino

There is a giant bird.

There is a giant bird in the wilderness.

There is a giant bird in the wilderness and it is dying, a life passing into the stillness of a desert canyon.

You descend. Water grows scarce. Everything is dusty: red and brown, red and brown.

At night, when the stars emerge, you lie on a ledge, thinking only of this bird you seek. In the morning, you cry as you hike. Picking your way through cliffs, the tears dry on your face, gluing windborne grit to your cheeks.

Your whole life is with you—all your memories, all your fears and joys— but it is distant. *I am no longer that person,* a voice says. *I am just this, just this hiking, just this hiking down.* Then the voice goes, the focus of your quest leaving it no room. You are wrapped in focus as you are wrapped in the canyon and wrapped in your aloneness. Pressing on, you struggle through the contorted land that somewhere holds the bird you've come to find.

Days pass, days slow. Late in a day that has blended and become one with all the others, you round a boulder. Here is the body. Pink sand. Feathers. Face beneath a wing. The moment finds you unprepared, as moments will.

Too late to turn around, to head back up through the maze of rock that squats between you and what you've left behind, you settle to the ground beside the giant bird. The setting sun glints on its hardest parts. You contemplate starting a small fire but do not rise to gather fuel. There are only rocks here anyway.

Sitting awake, waiting for dawn, the darkness gives birth to small ceremonies: singing, humming, piling pebbles, patterning dirt.

It is a long and shifting darkness.

When cold morning at last arrives, the sun hides behind canyon walls. You work to strap the bird to your spine, fastening the passed life to your beating, breathing, warming self. You smooth the ground where the bird once rested, where you drew those designs, resting together. You look at this smoothed place, unsure if it was ever otherwise, and begin to climb.

The climb takes time. You huff and sweat, burned by light, pushed by wind. You attend to your feet, to not falling, to establishing a pace that will carry you up and out of the wilderness. The weight tied to your back is forgotten. Your legs are strong. Your heart is ticking in your cracked lips when at last you reach the rim.

Sit. Recall your breath. Slouch. Spit. Stand again.

The life no longer lies dying or dead in the wilderness. It is with you, pressed to you. A faint trail is appearing, a path in this pathless world extending out from your body, which is bonded now and always to another.

This wasn't so hard, the voice says, the voice you haven't heard since setting out. It speaks falsely. It is a liar's voice. This was the hardest thing you've ever done.

Looking into the big blue sky beyond the canyon rim, the sadness comes up again, the body heavy on your own. Your lips are bleeding. Your legs feel weak.

Sit. Slouch. Feel the quiet violence of air moving against itself in all directions.

Take a drink.

Stand up again.

Watch the sky flow, flow, flow to fill the space from which a bird has flown.

Scrub Oak, Main Canyon

Cadence Summers

Even the trees
are dry this summer,
leaves curled and yellow,
as thin as shed skin,

and the bare upper limbs
of the scrub oak
scratch the cloudless sky
in supplication.

Swett Meadow

Cadence Summers

Listed ribcage,
nearly complete,
where the deer died
last winter.

Between the slats,
asters
shake their furled fists
at the warm blue sky
or sway
in open-handed constellations,
waiting—
for the blessing of the bees.

Snow Lake

Gail Folkins

I leaned against a warm boulder to offload the weight of my pack a moment. My friend, Rachel, stopped nearby to adjust her own pack. Amidst the unknowns of COVID-19, we were almost at the top of a ridge leading to Snow Lake in the Cascade Mountains. Part of the Alpine Lakes Wilderness, it was a pristine area long known to the Indigenous peoples who traveled the area for sustenance and trade. I'd made the trip in the daylight but never overnight. The trail, which began in shaded forest, transitioned to a rocky climb into the full sun of our first pandemic summer.

The trail narrowed around a corner, forcing me to angle sideways with my pack sticking out like a bright blue home. Rachel and I wore masks, as did most of the other hikers along the route. In the spring of 2020, Gov. Jay Inslee had shut down workplaces and businesses in the state of Washington due to the pandemic, but kept outdoor spaces open provided people followed best practices, including social distancing. Some of the hikers gave us an extra-wide berth, just in case. Despite the guidelines, it wasn't clear what might keep us safe.

Rachel and I debated whether to take the trip at all. Worried about her parents, who lived nearby, Rachel was torn between being careful and making the journey. After weighing our options, we decided to go ahead with some adjustments, like finding a destination a short distance away to eliminate stops for food and gas and minimizing the spread of the virus. Starting on a Sunday afternoon would help keep us away from early morning crowds. But even with our late weekend start, other hikers streamed past, albeit most on their way down.

The appeal of this trail and others in the region was easy to understand. Following the pandemic mandate, the rain-infused beauty of the nearby Cascades had taken on a new urgency as a site of recreation and escape. While a vaccine wasn't yet available, the outdoors as an emotional and physical antidote was.

A couple heading down waited for me to navigate another narrow turn. "Thank you," I said, the mask muffling my words. The pack I carried listed until I stepped sideways and caught up with it.

Rachel, the shoulder straps of her pack covered by two thick braids, turned toward another hiker heading down. Layered over his blue, short-sleeved shirt was a backpack. It was a clue that he, like us, was here for a longer trip.

"Hi, did you camp overnight?" Rachel asked.

The man nodded and swiveled toward us. His motion looked effortless despite the load he carried. "It was great," he said. "The moon came out."

Given the growing bank of clouds, we wouldn't be so lucky, even though the moon was close to full. I navigated another turn and felt the weight from the pack my brother had given me settle. A three-person tent and a groundsheet, also from my brother, filled much of the pack, along with food, water, some sweats to sleep in, and a can of wine. A sleeping bag, which hadn't fit with the rest of my supplies, bounced like a ball from where I'd tied it to the bottom of my pack.

Rachel covered ground in even strides without getting too far ahead.

"You can go faster," I said.

"I need to go slow for my back," Rachel said, although I wondered if it was for both of us.

Rachel, a well-versed backpacker, carried a load as large as mine, although it didn't seem to list, at least to my eye. Her hiking outfit of tights and a puffer coat appeared trim compared to my faded go-to hiking pants and rain jacket over a bulky but warm hoodie. Like me, Rachel carried a tent, along with her own set of COVID-19 worries. As part of our pandemic plan, we'd agreed to sleep in separate spaces to mitigate the risk.

"Even though you're the safest person to backpack with," Rachel said, meaning I'd already recovered from a mild-to-moderate case of COVID-19 earlier that spring.

"I hope so," I said. Antibodies or no, there was no telling if I might contract COVID-19 again. Without a vaccine, none of us were out of the woods, not yet, although escaping into them seemed like a good end-of-summer plan.

The afternoon warmed with overcast skies and a hint of humidity. During the final 500-foot ascent, I regretted the weight of the wine. The sleeping bag loosened from a ball to a shapeless form. Someone passed with their mask hanging off their face. We stopped at one of the last switchbacks to take in the ridge and mountain peaks behind us, including Bryant Peak, as a reminder we were almost there.

At this saddle between the ridge tops, an opening right before our descent, the stream of returning hikers slowed. Whether this meant people were headed home, or campers had already found their sites, I wasn't sure. Because the campsites were first-come, first-serve, finding a spot presented another uncertainty.

"They won't be as busy on a Sunday," Rachel said when we planned the outing. If the sites were taken by hikers who'd come a bit earlier or packed a little lighter, we'd have to swallow our disappointment and hike back until we reached the trailhead in light that lasted until 8 p.m. this time of year.

We stopped to let two men—maybe a father and teenage son—pass, all of us hesitating in an awkward dance of not knowing how much space to give. Rachel and I solved the issue by stepping off trail in a patch of loose rock to peel off our jackets while waving the pair on. Unwilling to stuff anything else into my pack, I tied my jacket around my waist.

Snow Lake appeared from between the trees like a blue-green bead. Viewing the lake, paired with the realization it was all downhill from here, eased my load. We paused at a few openings in the tree-lined slope to peer at the lake, just like the two men ahead of us kept doing. The craggy, exposed side of the ridge we'd just climbed, along with the pandemic, receded a little more into Douglas firs and spruce.

After a decline into the woods, one we'd need to hike upward after our trip was over, the trail transitioned from well-worn to smaller paths through the underbrush. While most of these led to the rocky lakeshore, a few wove toward campsites. We peeled off from the father and son duo with whom we'd traded places a few times along the way and focused on the campsites hidden along the shore.

"We'll look for my favorite," Rachel said. We walked faster, as if that would help us secure a spot. Through an opening in the underbrush, she pointed to a small rise surrounded by a Douglas fir grove. The lakeshore was a suggestion beyond the hill. We surveyed the site for any signs of others—a tent, a pack, even a ground sheet.

"It's free," Rachel said, in a mix of surprise and satisfaction.

A few other campsites were scattered beyond it, although the silence told us we were the only ones around. "Works for me," I said. Moonlight or not, we had a campsite.

Under the roots of the largest Douglas fir, I untied the jacket from my waist and slid off my pack. Searching through the blue bag, I found the ground sheet, thin and crackling as rice paper, and with Rachel's help spread it out in a square carpet for another layer of protection for the tent. The tent poles lengthened and bent together with ease. I pounded in the ground spikes, Rachel matched the tent hooks, and between the two of us the three-person dome, a tent my brother had not yet used, sprang to life.

"You have so much room," Rachel said. Easy as it would've been to share, we stuck with our two-tent plan.

"I'll store our extra things," I said, to make amends.

By the time I finished organizing the gear, Rachel had already pitched her yellow, cocoon-like tent with a doorway facing mine.

"It's on its last legs," she said. "But it'll work. Let's get some water." She grabbed her water bottle along with her own can of wine.

I stashed my ID, water bottle, and wine can in a day pack, which without the tent, sleeping bag, clothes, and food felt like nothing. On Rachel's heels, I wove through the trees and underbrush toward the reason we'd come here—the snow-fed lake.

The water stilled enough to reflect the peaks surrounding it, from Chair Peak to Kaleetan Peak to Mount Roosevelt. On the shoreline, the beach rocks felt smooth and cool. Only a few scattered voices rippled across the lake from day hikers hidden in the woods.

After hopping from one large rock to another, Rachel found a deep spot for the water purifier she'd brought. Between the two of us, we filled our containers and afterward came ashore to quench our thirst, not with our water but with our wine. The crack of my can made a loud, unexpected sound. "I wondered about carrying it," I said to Rachel, although the taste, even warmed, made a crisp reward.

"It's always a trade off," Rachel said.

Unsure if she meant the wine or the trip, I laid on the shore with hands behind my head. Like my body, my mind was free of the load we'd come up with—whether I'd be fit enough and slow Rachel down, if the uncertainties of a pandemic outweighed the escape.

Rachel lounged nearby, both of us still as the lake. The few voices nearby quieted, leaving only the water, mountaintops, and a few bats swooping. We stayed there awhile soaking in the silence of the shoreline and a sunset we couldn't see. The sky turned gray in increments so small we didn't notice the darkness until it was there to stay. Tentative raindrops touched our faces.

With our vision adjusting and headlamps to help, we found an opening through the underbrush toward the thin trail back to our campsite. We took off our boots, set them by our shared porch between the tents, and gathered our ready-made meals. I listened hard for anyone before deciding we were on our own.

Given the combination of a burn ban and summer warmth, we wouldn't build a campfire. Our entrees—freeze-dried macaroni and cheese for Rachel and an army-originated MRE (meals ready to eat) for me—would do. While my husband John and I had purchased a set of MREs for emergencies like earthquakes and flooding, a pandemic seemed as good a time as any to try one.

After pouring some of the lake water into the packet, I propped it against a rock. The packet to heat the food activated, with bubbles and steam pouring out like a small volcano. We finished our wine and watched, mesmerized as if it were a campfire.

"Yours is like a science experiment," Rachel said.

As the newbie on this trip, I was pleased to offer something. I peeled back the paper from the steaming spaghetti, while Rachel started on her mac and cheese. It was hard to say if the hike in made our meals taste better or if the food was already that good to begin with.

We sat across from one another in our tent doorways. The air was spiced with evergreen needles. I finished an apple cobbler dessert and stashed an energy bar for the next day. Headlamps pointed down, we put our utensils away before zipping up our tent fronts and calling it a night.

I read on my Kindle long enough to hear night birds calling and the tapping of rain. The journal I'd brought along, although not an essential item, felt vital in a different way. Writing an entry meant recording a journey characterized not by the ascent or physical difficulties, but by the uncertainties surrounding us, from how to mask and sanitize to how far we should stay apart.

Rachel's even breathing came from her tent. Rain meandered along the roof of mine. White flakes from the waterproofed seams collected on the tent floor. We'd selected the one wet night in August, meaning fall wasn't too far behind, along with a long pandemic winter. Though our timing might've been off, tonight the burden lightened. Droplets trailed down the rainfly, its thin sides an ample barrier.

Storm Over Beartooth Plateau

Eric le Fatte

These are rumblings of gods.
Clouds gather like assassins.
The wind has shed its empathy.
We heed the old advice:
stay low, find shelter,
get to the tent.
In the shufflings of millennia,
we've learned how to ruin a planet,
but cannot rule the hail and rain.
Under the cover of ripstop nylon,
we cross our fingers,
count the seconds,
and try to play cards
between canyons of thunder.
Lightning shatters the granite like glass.
Probability decides who survives.
We hope for the best,
but the elements
are not in our hands.

Crossing The River

Diane Gansauer

Long-distance backpacking involves facing fears. They might be rivers, wild animals, severe heights, snakes, insects, bad weather, lightning, hypothermia, running out of food, getting lost... But the river crossings in the Yellowstone Basin and south for about 40 miles presented a special conundrum for me. My first memory in life is of being tumbled into water by a rogue wave, along with my entire family. Subsequent events further embedded into my psyche a fear of rushing water.

Early in the year, I planned a hike of well over 400 miles along the Continental Divide Trail with my brother Mike. We would start far to the north in Montana, bearing south. I chose this direction rather than head northbound from the Wind River Range precisely to let those rivers in Yellowstone and along the Idaho border go down before I got there. All that careful planning was for naught when we got to arguably the most notorious crossing in the area: the South Buffalo Fork.

We were within three hours of the crossing and had waded the North Buffalo Fork without issue when it started to pour. The deluge lasted 45 minutes. My intrepid brother and I decided to stay in place in our rain gear and under additional cover from a tarp and trees, rather than slide down the muddy trail in the rain. In hindsight, we might have done better to continue, because when we got close to what we thought was a creek, it wasn't a creek anymore. We could hear a raging river in front of us when Mike turned to me and said, "I hope we're not going to have to cross that." The sound told us it was impassable.

A flash flood filled the river channel. Two hikers were on the other side. We hailed them, and the four of us shouted intel over the sound of the raging water. We learned that "just two hours ago" the water was calmly flowing at shin level when it started to rain there. To their regret, they hunkered down in their tents rather than cross. The river was now waist-deep and torrential.

Meanwhile, we were drenched and running out of food. Setting up camp was a study in re-purposing gear so we could stay as dry as possible through the night. We shifted tent layers, footprint, tarp, a log, and branches to create a shelter and crawled underneath, while a light rain continued intermittently. We had enough food for dinner, meager supplies for breakfast, and a few snacks, but that was about it. We needed to get to our re-supply point on the other side, 12 miles away at Brooks Lake Lodge, or we'd be in trouble.

Neither of us had any idea how long it takes for a flash flood to recede, but it didn't matter whether we knew or not. The situation was what it was, and we had no options but to settle down for the night and re-assess in the morning.

All night, a memory possessed me. Five years before, while hiking with my daughter and son-in-law in Glacier National Park, we had come to a pass after a pleasant morning of hiking. I peered around the corner to see what lay ahead, and blanched. There was a stiff headwind funneling through the notch at the pass, and a sharp three-thousand-foot drop beyond. The trail traversing the face was very narrow and in some parts missing. I turned to Zach, who was getting his lunch out of his pack, and said, "Put that back, we need to go." Startled, he asked, "Why, what's up?" My reply left no doubt. "If we stay here, fear is going to get the best of me. We need to go now." He packed up immediately. The three of us put on an additional layer, rounded the boulder we were sitting behind, and, with purposeful pace, faced into the wind and took off. I was in the lead and going at the top speed I could muster. "Mom!" my daughter shouted from behind. "You're practically running!" In a moment of insight, I yelled back, "I need to set the pace so the wind doesn't set it for me!" I braced the gusts, and Zach grabbed the lid buckle on my backpack as we jogged down the trail. With all of us leaning forward and angling one shoulder into the wind, he started singing. His rallying anthem of choice was the theme song from the adventure movie "Raiders of the Lost Ark." I started laughing. It was a brilliant diversion. You can't be afraid if you're laughing. It instantly became the family song for adventure.

All night, I contemplated that song, hoping to draw inspiration and lift my spirits.

We got up an hour later than usual, had breakfast, and slowly began to break camp. I kept humming my adventure theme. Then I decided to have a little chat with the river. The water was lower but still very fast. "Thank you for your effort, but we need more help," I whispered and walked back toward camp. It wasn't long before I heard voices and the clanking of trekking poles. Four strapping young men came striding down the trail very quickly, having just crossed over to our side and heading north. Their presence indicated crossing the river was possible now, but my mind wrestled with the physics. My body is much smaller and lighter than any of theirs. I was certain that the pack on my back was a higher percentage of my body weight, and knee-high water on them was definitely going to be higher on me. I would be a top-heavy reed on slippery rocks in a forceful current. We waited another hour before deciding we couldn't wait any longer if we wanted to get to Brooks Lake before dark, under conditions that at the least were going to be sloppy and slow and at the worst would include more rain.

We strung our boots on top of our packs and strapped on the strong sandals we'd brought for moments like this. Mike went ahead and was halfway across before I started. I was still humming until I waded in. My first steps into the cold water sent that cheerful song slipping away like broken branches in the flood.

The water topped at two inches above my knees. The bigger concerns were that it was fast and I couldn't see my feet, since the river was laden with mud. Deep in an old, cold, rushing fear of drowning, there was no room for error, no harbor for panic, nobody grabbing me from behind to make sure I didn't slip. There was only one option for moving forward and that was to face into the current, keep hold of my core, and choose my steps carefully but with purpose. I unbuckled my hip belt and dug my poles in just enough to secure each step. Keeping three points in contact with the river bottom as I side-stepped through the waves, I chose a different song. Barely audible over the roar, the old hymn "Guide My Feet, Lord" seeped up from years of religious upbringing and a life-long recognition of my humble status in the presence of Nature. Digging into a chasm of spirit, I sang, breathed deeply, and committed.

When I joined my brother on the other side, he already had his boots on and was ready to take off down the trail. I called out, "Mike, hold on a minute." I reminded him of my history with water. When he confessed he hadn't remembered that, I was glad (proud) he hadn't. "Give me a moment," I said. "I need to chat with the river."

Boots on, I turned back and walked to the edge, but this time I didn't have words. Instead, I gave the river a brief, wordless ritual of connection, helpful when words can't capture everything that's happened. I dug in a pole and bowed to the coursing water. Years of ingrained feelings didn't drop away at that moment, but they changed. Rooted in experience, principles for guiding my steps solidified. Walking through challenges requires preparation. Commitment. Awareness of the situation at hand. Regard for the river doing what a river does. Honest self-assessment. Care, not folly. Core strength beyond the physical.

My ability and resolve were tested by a force as pure in its objectives as a river, a powerful fellow traveler, and we each continued our paths. I felt a tempered respect replacing an old fear. I smiled, turned, and headed down the trail. And now and then, I sang.

Sensitive Fern as Sign
Onoclea sensibilis

Karina Lutz

A fat-lobed fern found in marshy areas,
along roadside ditches,
or forest edges with mosses and club mosses
(its ancient compatriots),
the sensitive fern slips spores through
liquid soil to disperse:
its presence says we are entering wetland
or former wetlands.
Sensitive fern is so named not because
it is sensitive to touch,
but because of the way it browns and curls
at the slightest frost,
as if pulling itself into itself,
as if to say, I can bear what follows.

What kind of medicine are you?
she asked, wordlessly, the way plants like it.
But no answer.

No medicine?—The herbalist's thought
cut her own silence like the rising of Braille
from the texture of clean bond,

                              then the thought of Braille
and who will learn it in an age of books-on-tape and
text-to-voice, and the sadness of the books in the library
holding flat memories of being loved by ones long dead

made her heart feel like a muscle again,
and before she knew it water came in
over the top edge of her short boots

and she looked back to see what treasures
she might have stomped
while thinking.

Now feeling—the rush of cold water along ankle—
and now sodden socks squish with each step.
A knee rises with nowhere to step but marsh flowers
and floating translucent lavender dragonfly eggs
and an opulence of brilliant medicines so stunning
she suspends her leg like that—

then gently pivots, to retrace the muddy puddles she made coming in.
Three steps and she returns to the sensitive ferns,
their fertile fronds upstanding as sentries
guarding, warning, or greeting:

Here is wetland. Welcome!
(now she registers
what she'd heard on the way in)

You have come to the right place. Tread lightly.

Goodbye, Steve

David Pratt

The day it happened was very cold, twenty below zero. There was a light breeze, and the sun was bright. Up here north of Lake Superior, that counted as a fine December day. The splashes of blood lay on the snow, a few paces apart. The bull moose was going strongly, the deep hoof prints evenly spaced, saplings to right and left bent like grass. It had been a long shot, but he should have downed it, or at least got off a second round. Poor bloody animal. If the bullet had gone low, the moose could not last long. If it had gone high, he could be in for a long hike.

The bush began to thin out. Steve came to the edge of a lake and saw the moose immediately, a good half-mile ahead, gaining ground, the great antlers thrust upward, moving fast across the ice. He crouched and took off his mitt. The cold metal of the Remington burned through his thin glove. He put the cross-hairs on the base of the animal's neck and fired. The moose did not react. He emptied the rest of the clip, without apparent effect. Then the huge animal was into the bush on the opposite shore.

Follow, or leave it? If Jeff had been with him, they wouldn't have hesitated. But Jeff had called at six that morning to cancel because his wife was sick, and on his own this was going to be a challenge. The moose looked like it could go a long way. It was illegal to abandon a kill, but who would ever know? The tracks and bloodstains would be blown over by tomorrow, bears and wolves would devour the carcass, and raccoons and crows would pick the skeleton clean. But it was the end of the hunting season, and you didn't draw a moose license every year. He checked his GPS. He was still only a mile from his truck. It was just after noon. Not a cloud in the sky. If he did catch up with the moose, he would need plenty of time to field-dress the meat. Okay, he'd follow for an hour, make a fire, eat the lunch Karen had packed for him, then turn back.

He pulled up the hood of his orange parka and tied the drawstrings. Out on the ice, the wind made his eyes water, and the tears froze in his eyelashes. But the snow was packed, and he could move quickly. This was where the $300 high-tech aluminum snowshoes paid off. Just as well he hadn't brought Jason with him; it would be too much for an eight-year-old. In a couple of years, his son could come grouse hunting with him. So long as he got joint custody. That was the key to everything. As a rule, they did fun stuff together on Saturdays, but today he'd dropped the boy off for hockey practice at 6:00 a.m. Karen would pick him up on her way home from the graveyard shift at the hospital. He needed today for thinking. The last three months had been a struggle between excitement and guilt, and guilt had been winning. Now that he knew what he really wanted, there was no further justification for deception. So he would tell Karen. Tomorrow.

Now he noticed that bloodstains had begun to show on both sides of the tracks. One of his last shots must have hit. He reached the bank. The gradient was too steep for snowshoes, and he unbuckled them. He slung the rifle behind his back and climbed the slope, grabbing bushes and saplings for support. From the churned-up snow on the hillside, it seemed that the moose had been struggling too.

He paused to catch his breath, turned, and looked back over the lake he'd crossed. On the far shore, white birches stood out against the dark cedar and jack pine. The snow was pristine, frost and icicles sparkling in the trees. He loved this land, had been born in Kapuskasing, where his father was a Baptist minister, and where he'd grown up hunting, fishing, and canoeing. He loved his son. He loved Suzanne.

He must have loved Karen, years ago, when they were first married and moved up north. They were good years, although at the time the sixty-hour weeks had seemed exhausting. When he'd taken over the elementary school, it was a zoo. Older kids guarding the washrooms and charging the younger ones a dime to use them. A couple of teachers so unpopular that the kids used to piss on the windscreens of their cars in winter until they were coated with half an inch of yellow ice. Now the school was regarded as the best in the district. He was popular with his staff and well regarded in the town. Some of the friends he and Karen shared would take sides, but neither of them would lose their status in the community.

He resumed his way up the incline, and as soon as the ground leveled out, he saw the moose. It had stopped in a stand of sumac some eighty meters ahead. It was standing still, the head with its massive antlers drooping. Conscious of the beating of his heart, he unslung the rifle and raised it very slowly. The breeze was in his face, and the moose had not seen him. He took a couple of breaths, exhaled most of the third, then slowly squeezed the trigger. The shot hit square in the shoulder. The moose made no sound; its head came up as its body began to sink. Then it crumpled into the snow. Hoo-ya! This was why you hunted!

He'd previously shot only one moose; this one was much bigger. Tomorrow was Sunday, and he would come out with a couple of guys on snowmobiles to fetch the carcass. They'd be happy to do it for fifty pounds of meat. The moose was lying on its side. Steve advanced on it slowly. The eyes were open, and he touched one of them lightly with the tip of his rifle. There was no reaction. He pulled the mouth open. A small gust of animal breath hit him in the face. Little wear on the back molars: probably a three-year-old. He found his tape and measured the rack: 54 inches tip to tip. It would be something to have the head mounted. But that was out of the question, he was going to need every dollar for the next year or two. He wrote down the GPS reference in his notebook and took three pictures with his phone.

He unsheathed his knife and cut a line from the crotch to the tip of the sternum, holding the blade upwards with his fist inside the animal, to avoid perforating the intestines. He freed the colon by cutting around the anus and tied it off with a piece of string. The warmth of the intestines kept his hands from freezing. He left the scrotal sac intact and attached the game seal to a nearby tendon after notching out the month, date, and time of kill. He cut around the diaphragm, carefully freed the windpipe at the throat, and severed the attachments of the internal organs. Then, taking care not to puncture them, he pulled the hundredweight of entrails out on to the ground. The full stomach was bigger than a basketball. The blue-grey pile steamed in the cold. He took paper towels from his pack and wiped out the inside of the carcass.

He worked fast, forcing himself to slow down every time he felt a sweat beginning. He cut out the tongue, wrapped it in paper towels, and put it in his pack. Karen would appreciate that. Now he was left with a carcass that looked as though it weighed five or six hundred pounds. No way he could hang all of that; he didn't have enough time or enough rope. There was a white pine a few steps away with a branch twelve or fifteen feet up. He had a hundred feet of quarter-inch nylon rope, perhaps enough to hang the hip and sirloin. He cut the tenderloins free from inside the rib cage, wrapped them, and put them in his pack. He slung the rope over the branch and hauled up the two pieces of sirloin. Each leg weighed seventy or eighty pounds, and he had to divide them in two. He had just enough rope. Too bad to have to leave the rest of the carcass for the critters, but they'd go for the liver and heart first, the meat would freeze fast, and with luck there would be plenty left by the time he got back tomorrow. The pieces hanging from the tree looked bizarre; he took a couple more pictures.

He built a fire quickly, placing it so that he could sit on the remains of the still-warm moose to eat his lunch. He unscrewed the thermos top and poured soup into the cup. Thick pea soup. Even better flavor than usual, maybe a new spice. Karen was one hell of a cook, he'd say that for her. She'd be all right. Had a good job, knew how to manage her money.

Had adapted well to the north. And smart—smarter than him, he'd always known that. A hard worker, too, like himself.

Perhaps that was part of the problem. They'd striven so long and so hard to build a future that they'd worked the joy out of their marriage. Summer after summer, never taking a decent vacation, she taking a graduate degree in nursing, he earning his principal's ticket. Everything had become routine between them. Their relationship had always been sensible and logical. Until he'd met Suzanne, he hadn't known what passion was. He and Karen didn't even talk much anymore. Would the future have been ever-increasing boredom right into old age? Well, now he had the chance to start over. It would be different this time. Suzanne wanted kids. That was okay, he'd always hoped for more than one.

In addition to the soup, there were two chicken sandwiches. He unzipped the plastic bag. The bread was cold to the touch. Then he saw the envelope. It had been between the two sandwiches. He stared at it. It was sealed. He tore it open, and unfolded a small sheet of paper:

"Goodbye, Steve."

That was all. He was transfixed, paralyzed for a moment by a chaos of thoughts and emotions. He had been chilled, now he broke into a sweat. Goodbye Steve. Well, she wasn't home when he left that morning; she just meant *Have a good day*. No way. Goodbye—she knew! How in hell?

Would she be gone when he got home? My God, would she have taken off down east with Jason? The thought was unbearable. She had her own car, and there was a train out at noon. Oh my God, could this be a suicide note? No, no way, never, she was not that type. Then he thought, Goodbye—maybe she's poisoned the food! That different flavor in the soup. What was that burning sensation in his stomach? She must have access to all kinds of poison at the hospital. No, he was being irrational, that was not believable. He opened the sandwiches. They looked normal. He threw them in the fire.

She couldn't know! He'd agreed with Suzanne: no letters, no phone calls, no emails, no appearances together in public. No perfume, even. They saw each other only when the Principals' Council met in Thunder Bay. You knew a thing or two about deception if you were a preacher's kid.

It had to be a joke. Or perhaps she did know, and this was an attempt to bring him to his senses. Anyway, get home fast, find out what was going on. If she'd gone, my God, "His wife has left him," would be all around the school by noon on Monday. Instead of the admiring, "He got his moose."

He had been thinking of roasting a piece of meat, but now he packed up quickly and left the fire burning. During the short break, the perspiration in his clothes seemed to have frozen. His undershirt felt not clammy but icy. He checked his watch. There were still two hours of daylight, and he was less than an hour from the truck. The miniature thermometer attached to the slider of the zipper on his parka now read 25 below. With his knife, he cut blazes into the trunks of surrounding trees and some more when he reached the edge of the ice. Then he buckled on his snowshoes and followed the tracks back across the lake. He set himself a moderate pace, enough to get warm, not enough to raise a sweat.

Once off the ice, there was no need to follow the tracks, which in any case were becoming covered by lightly drifting snow. He had been heading south until he shot the moose, which had taken off eastward. The direct route to the truck would be the fastest, the third side of the triangle. He checked his GPS: 1.6km.

The going was hard, harder still where the brush was thick. At times, his snowshoes sank in the snow more than a foot. But without them, one would be exhausted in a hundred yards. He was moving up a steady gradient. The light ahead indicated a break in the trees, probably a lake. It was a lake all right, a small one, but he had come out at the edge of a forty-foot cliff.

He looked furiously to right and left for a descent. Slow down, slow down, he told himself. Start getting frustrated and you end in trouble. If he'd still had the rope, he could have tied it to a tree and rappelled straight down. It looked as though the best route was to follow the cliff-top eastward until the land dropped to the lake. There was no path, and the ground was steep and broken, but here the snow had blown off the high ground, so he took the snowshoes off and carried them. At its lowest point, the shore was four feet above the lake. He took a good grip on his rifle and the snowshoes, jumped down to the surface, and went right through the ice.

The shock of the cold water was stunning. But it wasn't deep. He went in only to his thighs. He gasped and clambered out. He cursed his stupidity. He should have tested the ice. An underwater current or a beaver hole was always a risk near shore. He crawled to firmer ice and knelt for a moment trying to catch his breath. He rolled over a couple of times, so the snow could wick some of the moisture from his clothes. His right leg was hurting, and when he stood up, it buckled. He'd twisted his knee.

He felt an unfamiliar sensation, like a tiny ice-cold ball bearing at the bottom of his stomach. Deep breath. You can do this, Steve. Leaning on his rifle, he got to his feet again, then slowly put weight on the bad knee. It hurt like hell, but he could handle it. At least his mitts had stayed dry. He sat down, took off his rubber hunting boots, and emptied the water. His wet socks began to freeze, no point in trying to squeeze them out. He was beginning to shiver. He pulled the boots back on, reattached his snowshoes, and moved off across the lake.

He couldn't feel much below his knees. But his legs still carried him strongly, and after a while some sensation returned. Just cold, he told himself, no frostbite. Move steadily and trust to good circulation. His vehicle had a powerful heater and was now no more than half a mile away. The light was beginning to fade. The snow no longer sparkled.

It was heavy going through the bush. Two or three times, his snowshoes caught on a branch under the snow, pitching him forward and causing a searing pain in his knee. But his navigation was good. The GPS and compass brought him out to the logging road a dozen paces from his truck.

He allowed himself to feel cold, anxiety, fatigue, and relief only when he plunked into the seat. He turned the key in the ignition. The starter cranked and did not fire. He floored the accelerator and tried again.

At home and at school, he kept the block heater plugged in, but the vehicle had been sitting now for some six hours. Cursing, he opened the hood, took off a mitt, and removed the air filter. His violent shivering made every action difficult. He sprayed starter fluid into the carburetor, replaced the filter, turned the key again. For a moment, he thought it was going to fire. "Start, you bastard!" he screamed. He kept trying until the battery began to fade and the sun dropped over the horizon.

He took the cell phone from the glove compartment, began to dial his home, then stopped and dialed Jeff's number. The display said, "No service."

He got out of the car, raised his rifle in the air, and fired three shots. Paused. Three more. Paused. Three more. The echoes died, and the silence surged back, followed by the distant sound of a wolf howling. There were no answering shots. No one was out here, no one was looking for him.

He was beginning to feel a deep cold, a lassitude in his limbs, an inability to think sharply. He was thirsty, and the bottle of water in his pack was frozen solid. Before leaving home, he'd left a note for Karen, saying where he was going, but no one else knew.

He tried to review his options calmly. He had his Arctic sleeping bag and emergency foil blanket. He could stay with the truck, build a fire, and walk out in the morning. He could build a snow house, which would be warmer than the cab of the truck. With the meat in his pack, he even had food.

Rule number one was, stay with your vehicle. And he would have done so, if it had not been for his son. He simply had to find out whether Jason was still at home or at least confirm that Karen had not left town with him. The logging road ran south at a narrow angle from the highway. How far had he driven in? Five miles? Eight miles? Or he could bushwhack straight through to the highway. His compass would take him there: it couldn't be more than a mile. Say half an hour. There were always people driving back to town on Saturday evening from weekend sales at the Lakehead. He could be home less than two hours from now.

He took a flashlight from the glove compartment. It had plenty of juice. He caught his reflection in the mirror and saw a yellow patch the size of a quarter on his cheek. Frostbite. No time to deal with it now. It was painless so long as it was frozen.

Writing with difficulty, he left a note saying, "Truck won't start, heading north to highway." It seemed to take for ever to get the snowshoes back on. He left his rifle and his pack in the car. Three hundred meters into the bush, he knew he should have followed the road. No point in turning back now. He had to clamber over fallen trees. His clothes were covered in snow. He checked his compass every few steps. The light from the flashlight reflected back from the snowflakes now beginning to fall. All his limbs felt twice their normal weight. Get to the highway. *Goodbye Steve,* what on earth did she mean? Get to the highway. He had stopped shivering. He barely bothered to move saplings aside, ignoring the beating they gave his face.

The third time he fell he lay a few moments and wondered whether he was going to get up again. It seemed easier just to stay there. But then the image of her face came into his mind, with her level, friendly, encouraging gaze. Not Suzanne. Karen. He said her name aloud. He struggled to his feet. It was not too late. He just had to get to the highway.

He tripped again almost immediately. With half-frozen fingers, he unbuckled the snowshoes and abandoned them. Now he was limping through snow up to his thighs. His clothes, icy with frozen moisture, no longer provided insulation. His breath came in gasps, and the freezing air burned his throat. At one moment he thought he was on the highway. Then he was at home, sitting with his wife at the dinner table. He was in bed with pneumonia, Karen's cool professional hand on his brow. He was saying goodbye to Jason at the rink, the boy hugging his neck and saying enthusiastically, "Good luck, Dad!"

Jason. Karen. The highway. Go straight. Get to the highway. Due north. Don't stop. He seemed to have been walking for hours. For years. He was falling more frequently now, as much from exhaustion as from tripping.

And he did get to the highway. Had there been witnesses, they would have seen a figure, shambling like a bear, with the clumping gait of frozen feet, holding a fading flashlight, nose and cheeks frostbitten, blood frozen on his face from the slashes of branches, mumbling to himself, eyes red-rimmed and staring. They would have seen this apparition emerge from the trees on the south side of the highway, stagger across, and plunge straight into the bush on the opposite side, still heading north.

What if I can't get home?

Santa Fe, above 10,000 feet

Nicole Grace

Perhaps it was the thin air or
dew misting
off blinding snow,

the hours-long crunch
of boots into a
mantra, swooning me

in the vastness, in my
aloneness, a lone person
in a sea of swaying bark,

when I saw the absurdity
of the idea of aloneness,
how I was the wildness

I was breathing in, the ice
chandeliering off pine needles,
rabbit prints in the frost.

I had come here to not feel
what was troubling me but
I would leave knowing

escape was not necessary,
the wilderness was always
in me, chanting along

every footstep here or
anywhere. I made my way
back down, but not out,

my face crisp as paper
birch fanned against an
immaculate blue sky.

The North Fork, 2017

Emmy Savage

> *All the shadows of the dark cannot keep*
> *the sun from rising.* Tom Renaud

It is the fourteenth of June and this would have been my wedding anniversary; we would have been married forty-three years. I cast a quick mental glance over the landscape of loss, trauma, and difficult choices that have landed me here. But regret is tempered, and I give thanks that I am walking in the Sangre de Cristo Mountains under a smoldering sky, so blue it is almost purple and, at mid-day, many shades darker than the mountain peaks.

It has been a hard slog getting here to our camp: four creek crossings, three that necessitated removing my boots and replacing them with water shoes. The water is only a few degrees warmer than ice, and I feel shocked into a new energy level each time I plunge across the current.

I wasn't anticipating doing this hike so early in the season and without better preparation. I am carrying a tent, two sleeping bags—one for my constant companion and whip-smart red heeler Sarah—a bear-proof food container that weighs way more than it should, warm clothes, three quarts of my well water, iodine pills, hiking poles, an inflatable mat, E.M. Forster's *A Room with a View,* a pen, a small pocket journal, and dog food. After several days of thunderstorms, the forecast was for a whole week with no storms or mayhem, and I seized the opportunity: Bag Woman and Wonder Dog take to the hills.

At first, I found my pack to be so heavy and the weight so poorly distributed that it took my breath away. After several stops to reposition, things improved; by lunchtime I had drunk one of my quarts of water, so that helped lighten the load.

The first creek crossing is really a small gorge with a bridge made up of slender logs that wobble in tandem in such a way as to make relatively safe footing. The bridge is high enough above the torrent of snowmelt that it stays dry. Otherwise, if the logs were wet, it would be much more treacherous.

At this point, the North Fork Trail turns up the mountain to the left and switches back through a young aspen forest. Something happened here, probably an avalanche. The forest floor is strewn with deadfall, and the new trees are all of the same vintage. We climb and climb before coming to our second crossing. I test the sapling bridge, but find the logs to be too slick for me. The creek water boils up against a dam of logs and debris, and I worry Sarah will get slammed against it. I try to coax her up onto the bridge or at least into the shallower water. But she is having none of my interference. She launches herself into the deep water and immediately the current takes her up against the dam. While she dog paddles, the current forms a backwash and she is able to float into a calm space. The rest is easy. Sarah looks like a red and white muskrat emerging from the creek, wet to her gunwales. A good shake puts things to rights. After I wade across in my water shoes, we sit waiting for my feet to dry before I put them back into my boots.

As we start our next ascent, the aspen leaves quake in the breeze and create a shimmering motion across the forest floor. Walking here feels like walking under water. The next crossing will be the most formidable. I don't know how I will get Sarah across. The water is deep and roiling mad, and there is no dam this time to rest against, only a waterfall at the edge of the crossing that might bring on broken bones, if not worse.

I decide to carry Sarah across, and it is a struggle hefting a forty-pound dog. I think she realizes the gravity of the situation and stops wiggling as I step out into the thigh-high water. I am cautious to place each foot between boulders and on the firm creek bottom while pushing my way against the current. When I arrive at the opposite shore, I put Sarah down and tell her to sit and to stay. But wonder dogs have minds of their own, and when I arrive at the opposite shore to retrieve my pack and poles, I look down and see her standing next to me.

"Oh, Kiddo," I say. "I guess you're on your own this time." We cross again. This time Sarah leaps from one submerged rock to the next, and I watch my footing as I balance my ergonomic disaster of a pack. We cross safely and not too long after, the trail breaks out into a long sloping valley surrounded by thirteen-thousand-foot peaks. We stop to admire the view and to eat our lunch. Columbine flowers are usually thick here, but it is too early in the season and their buds are still tightly furled. The last creek crossing is coming up and then there will be steep climbing before we come to the upper valley where we'll camp.

When we arrive at the upper valley, I am bushed, and as soon as I can, I head off trail in search of level, dry ground. I find a camp spot next to a beautiful, healthy Engelmann spruce. It is windy, but I am too tired to search for a more sheltered place. I pitch the tent and spread out our sleeping bags. I don't mind that the tent is facing directly into the sun. We will need to absorb all the heat we can before nightfall when the temperature will go down into the low thirties, if not lower.

A few puffy clouds gather, and one blocks the sun. The whole valley with its circling mountains instantly goes dark. I hope we can get through the night without bears eating us or our freezing to death. Sarah is so trusting. She doesn't look at me as if to say, "We could be home now. We could be watching Netflix and Dog TV. We could be eating supper and then sleeping in our own cozy beds."

Tomorrow we will climb up to the cirque at the base of Venable Pass and take the fork to the north on the Rito Alto-San Isabel Trail. After the initial climb of about a thousand feet, the trail will level out as we walk into the spare and sober beauty of the alpine.

I sleep fitfully and become aware that the tent is no longer dark. But this thin light isn't the light of dawn or daybreak. There is a half-moon in the sky above our doorway, and the pale light makes me think we have at least two more hours before daybreak. I have to pee, but it is cold, and I lie in my sleeping bag thinking about the things I must do before we leave in the morning. I know that the temperature must be in the thirties or high twenties, because the temperature goes down to forty-five at my house, two thousand feet below. Though I tucked Sarah in before we went to sleep, she doesn't seem to have the sleeping bag knack. She is unmoored from the bag and lies tightly curled in a shivering ball at the bottom of the tent. I fold the bag over and mound it up on top of her. She doesn't budge.

Around six, I hear barking coming from the valley we passed through yesterday. (When I get home, I comb the internet for barks: wolverines, badgers, bears, weasels, foxes?) I later determine the barking to be a fox giving a warning cry. He is alerting the whole valley: "Strangers in our midst!"

In this vast and empty space, there is the sense we are being watched. Of the usual suspects—marmots, foxes, bears—I will only see the marmots in their sleek red-brown coats lumping across the rocks after the sun comes up. And when she wakes, Sarah will bark at them and let them know: "Come into our territory at your peril." Marmots can tear up a tent, so I am glad Sarah will set boundaries, which I hope they'll respect while we're gone today.

But right now, it is still grey and the mass at the bottom of the tent isn't moving. I decide to venture out into the cold, dark world of rushing water and silence. I walk down toward the creek to pull the bear bag with our food out of a spruce where I hung it the night before and notice a rime of frost on the grass. I have to push my way through waist-high willows to find a smaller tributary creek, one that originates out of

Groundhog Basin. (Groundhog? Did some well-meaning person mistake marmots for groundhogs when they named this place?)

I fill my water container from a tiny waterfall, where the creek is surrounded with globe flowers and marsh marigolds in bloom. Upslope, sunlight is catching the very top of the peak above us. I watch the light move down the mountain, slowly, slowly. Will the sun's tide ever reach us? I walk up to greet it and, stepping into the light, feel it wrap me in warmth. As I begin to bask, here is Sarah. How did she know it was safe to get up? We linger in the sunshine and wonder at the difference between cold and warmth, darkness and light, menace and joy.

Everything seems to take longer this morning: hanging bear bags, brushing teeth away from camp in case a bear fancies the smell of toothpaste, treating water with iodine pills, packing the day pack with provisions and warm clothes, zipping up the tent. When I am finally finished, we set out on the trail we left yesterday and start the one-thousand-foot ascent to the Rito Alto-San Isabel Trail.

Yesterday, I saw one very large bear paw print in the mud at one of the creek crossings and two large mounds of scat. I also noted that we were following a horse and a size-twelve boot. We never see the bear, the hiker, or the horse, but they have added their spirit vibrations to the place.

At Mass, our priest Father Eric often asks for the grace to see God in all things. I ask myself if I see God here in the glory of these mountains and the creeks that cascade down the slopes at almost vertical angles. Or if I feel God's presence in the wet ground and the flowers and the water-sound echoing off the rocks. Maybe I do; maybe that is what draws me here. But in the moment, I am more aware of my fatigue and my fear when the sun goes down. Clearly, I am not ready to walk through the valley of the shadow and fear no evil.

The climb this morning is steep, and I am surprised at how fatigued I am from yesterday's hike. But this is one of the loveliest passages in the Sangres; as the trail moves up through spruce groves and out into open rock and grass and flowers, it rises above tree line and into the true alpine. When we arrive at the fork, we are at eleven thousand feet. The sun at this elevation is so bright and unfiltered that colors vibrate with life, and the sound of falling water and silence merge.

We catch our breaths and set out to the north, up into the valley where lie the headwaters of the North Fork of North Crestone Creek. Peaks circle us. Sedimentary rock that was once horizontal has been uplifted to forty-five-degree angles, augmenting a sense of vertigo shimmering at the edge of things. We continue across snowfields frozen hard enough to hold our weight and through melt in the trail that still has a skin of ice from last night. At this altitude, I see American pipits wagging their tails and white-crowned sparrows who favor alpine terrain with their lovely song. Even a pair of mountain bluebirds wheels beneath our feet as we look over the edge of the trail.

As we round into a new cirque, we can see the San Isabel Pass where the trail disappears into massive snowfields. Somehow, I haven't got the energy or my microspikes to tackle these snows or the ambiguity of the trail's course through difficult terrain. I try to make out the trail as it slants up towards the pass and disappears into another field of snow. I decide to turn around. But despite my fatigue, I feel confident I will return. I'm growing more comfortable walking this close to the sun and besides, Sarah loves snow.

We are back from our hike and today is the Feast of Corpus Christi, the day we strew dried flowers as we proceed into Nada's chapel, and Father Eric tells us that "matter matters, and that the word is made flesh."

When I think of the "word made flesh," I always think of Thoreau's pickerel. "Ah, the pickerel of Walden," he writes, and tells us how, for him, these beautiful fish, flecked with gold and green and blue and spots of black, are the very essence of Walden Pond, with its moods and ruffles, its clarity and cold, its blue and white and green moments, its sand and granite, all distilled into this one beautiful fish. Wild strawberries will also do this for me. As I crush their small, firm bodies with my tongue, they burst with the essence of sunlight, blue sky, columbine, melting snow, red conglomerate, and rushing water. But on our hike to the Rito Alto-San Isabel Trail, strawberries were still flowers, and the willow leaves at eleven thousand feet were still tightly closed. The essence of this hike was, for me, bending over a small rivulet in a field of white and yellow globe flowers and catching water in a bottle. Distilled in that memory are the sky and the peaks, the sounds of rushing water and the marmot's shrill cries and the barking fox, cloud shadows, and sunlight washing down a mountainside, pushing away the darkness and warming the earth.

I will admit to being afraid on this hike. It was the first time I had camped alone in the Sangres, and at such high altitude, hours and miles away from help or human comfort. During the day, there is plenty to occupy my mind with tasks that must be accomplished. And as long as there is sunlight, I can keep fear at bay. I can put one foot in front of the other. I can even distract myself, when the chores are completed, with a book I love. But looking back, I think I was not the only being that was vulnerable in that landscape. All beings that live there are vulnerable, even the landscape itself. And this realization feels like a spiritual step into unchartered ground, into a new way of being, into a compassionate embrace that is as large as mountains. This compassion comes from within me, not from without. It is possible that the North Fork, for all its darkness and scary sounds, its phantom bears and barking foxes, has taught me that we experience God's presence not from without, but from within.

Author's Note: This essay is dedicated to Sarah, who died April 8, 2022.

© 2022 by Andie Thrams

Double Diamond

Margaret Pettis

Throwing a diamond hitch
over the canvas manty,
she snugged the load
with her boot heel set
in the mule's tough hide.
The stiff rope bristled
through her doeskin glove
like a snake backing
out of a hole.

Cinchas tight, the mules lined out
in a quick circle behind her horse—
eight outstretched necks,
each black tail knotted
to the next mule's halter rope.
Flies plagued ears, furry
as hellebore, bitter with salt
from trailing up the pass
through shotgun hail
and forked lightning.
She sang to them
up the switchbacks.

At dusk on Queen's River
she belled the Judas mule
and hobbled the renegades
on a buzzing carpet of lupine,
buttercup, and mallow.
She draped sweat-foam blankets
to air on the sawbucks
perched on a downed ponderosa.
She built a small fire,
let it burn down to coals,
smoke drifting
through cones
toward Orion.

Slipping a pine wand
into the chipped enamel
kettle, she freed a puff
of steam up the steep
black chimney of spruce.
No need for a tent tonight.

Between sips of chamomile,
fingers tacky with pitch,
she idly practiced knots
on a hank of soft manila:
squaw hitch, buckle,
double Dutchman, honda.

Teasing coyotes,
she unleashed the high notes
of a dented harmonica,
played glittery glee
to the stars.

Hooters

Laura Girardeau

They call us Hooters, but we're far from waitresses in short shorts. We're guardians of the ancient forests. We hoot endangered spotted owls down from the trees. Our uniform is lace-up boots, flannel shirts and orange vests that hold the tools of our trade: a compass, an aerial photo showing the oldest trees' rounded tops, and live mice to tempt the owls. We're perfumed with the scent of cedar and the sulfur of off-the-map hot springs. We have no use for mirrors, and we've never felt more gorgeous.

In the backwoods bars, there's a price on our heads. Loggers hang owls in effigy over the door. They think we stole their jobs, but ancient forests are like emeralds. If you mine too many, they're gone forever (owls or not), along with the jobs. They post signs that say, "I Like Spotted Owls—Fried" and "Hooters Go Home."

We're already home. We live in deep wild, where rivers are birthed. Up the trail, the mighty McKenzie emerges from a lava tube. At Blue Hole, it spills out in turquoise surprise, playing "I Spy" on our work with its all-knowing eye. We think the river approves.

It's hard to believe we get paid for this. We're ready to risk-'n-roll. The Forest Service taught us how to drive our rigs into ditches to dodge logging trucks, avoiding the cliffs. They told us to "curse our fall" if we plummet from a huge log onto the sharp jumble below. They say swearing expels air from your lungs and boosts your chances of survival. But we want to fall, into this wild life.

They taught us how to avoid getting lost. How to use a compass to escape a fortress of trees when their crowns block the sun. Our boss got lost once, called us on her radio to tell us where to pick her up. "I'm in a clear-cut," she laughed. That's all she knew. The Oregon forests are a chessboard of clear-cuts. We're pawns hopping across the board, trying to become queens.

We see the chessboard on the aerial photos we use as maps. Only a few cathedrals remain, tiny Emerald Cities. The trees stand proud like our foremothers, telling their stories in sun slants. Their skin is cinnamon and butterscotch, both rough and soft. Their canopy swallows light like a black hole, turns everything deep green. I want to get lost in Oz.

A hundred feet up these trunks is the treasure: a nested pair. The nest tree is the motherlode. If we find it, we save a mile of forest around the tree. Thanks to the Endangered Species Act, the logging trucks and bulldozers can't go there. Like green witches, we draw circles of protection around eternity. But first, we must find evidence of love. Only nested pairs are protected.

So we hoot the wild down from the treetops in its own language. We cup our hands and give four throaty barks at just the right cadence. We place a live pet-store mouse on one cinnamon trunk. Its pink candy eyes are too bright to resist. The forest holds its breath.

Then an owl flies down from its silent skyscraper, in a spotted cloak to match the dappled light. If it's a mated male, he carries the mouse to the female and gives her the gift, like a true gentleman. If they're a nested pair, she flies to the nest tree to feed the babies first.

We fly through the forest too, scaling mazes of blown-down logs to follow her. The trees take a bite out of us. Our knees and elbows bear scars, landmarks for our someday granddaughters. If we're lucky, we get there in time to see talons and tail disappear into one chosen tree. A tree that's been here since Columbus got us into this mess.

We mark the tree, and we've done it. We've saved the pair's fragile love, along with a mile of forest around it, for one more season.

But more often than not, we know love is up there, but can't find the nest. So we go back, off the road, off the clock. We do anything to find them. We strap on skis and hoot under the full moon at midnight. We shift our schedules to owl time, listening for nature's call-back. We lay our camping mattresses down on soft duff or hard gravel, and wait.

When we get the call in deepest night, we take a compass-bearing on hope. At dawn, we follow the bearing and "mouse" the owls. When they lead us to the mother tree, we mark it with an *X* for wild. This is the center of Nature's mile now.

This is the place your bulldozer jaws can't reach. We are the women your jaws can't reach. Your owl on a noose above the bar only stokes our fire. We've tossed out the maps and navigate with our hearts. We follow the scent of cedar to soak in secret hot springs that only Hooters know.

In a mossy cave, steam rises from the earth and dissolves our walls. Underwater, our sore muscles stand out like burnished hills. Our thighs are bronze, strong ladyhood. We've grown branches. In the hot pool, we loosen our limbs to lush. The roar of the river is all we hear.

Then, across miles and centuries, a spotted owl calls in four throaty barks. Not because we called. Just because. That's when we praise our fall into the wild.

Author's Note: The northern spotted owl inhabits old-growth forests in the Pacific Northwest and is an important indicator species. In the early 1990's, it gained protection under the Endangered Species Act, and logging in national forests with nested pairs was halted by court order. This helped protect pockets of a threatened ecosystem, but created controversy in the logging industry. Changing administrations led to changing protections, and the invasive barred owl now competes for habitat. The species is still in decline, but if you venture far from a road, deep into an emerald forest, you may hear its call.

© 2022 by Andie Thrams

Refuge

Ian Ramsey

As permafrost softened
and parts per million surged
and lawyers circled the oil rigs,
I followed the ancient hoof grooves
across the tundra, stumbling over tussocks
in a small city of caribou, through the huntings
of wolves and the sunblind grizzlies and three-day-old
wobbling calves, and went deep, wherever that was, into
the hard calloused body that ancestors lived inside, into migrations
across land where bones were broken and fires mysterious and priorities
failed and politics failed and there was only the big, raw, hard unrelenting earth.
The nightless, treeless, arctic landscape was part cave painting and part slushy taiga,
calamitous feedback loop of the collapsing thermodynamic vault that was existential threat.
A thousand miles west of my monkish truancy, an obsessed scientist was gathering reindeer.
Herding musk oxen. Bison and wild horse hooves regrassed Beringia to lock in carbon,
with rusty Soviet tanks mimicking ten-ton mammoth trample to deepen the once
permanent underturf freeze. There were Harvard geneticists shaping elephant
helices into a mammothish fetus inside a birthing tank, the first of a herd.
Was the gulag ark a Jurassic punchline or a better bet than seeding
the atmosphere with aerosols? The ravenous microbial swarm
hung heavy with mosquitoes, grant money, and cold-resistant
hemoglobin. Between the deep past and the future, a man
sits in a grassy valley. Pleistostalgia or futureproofing?
The answer grazes the hot, wet stomachs of large
herbivores and the collapsing sinkholes of taiga.
The earth forgives itself for the long valleys
of drought, the axes of ice, the windows
of biotic flourishing and scarcity,
the shifts. Now the deep past.
Now the narrow passage
to the deep future.
The now is long.

Geotraumatics

Ian Ramsey

High in the Arctic,
I ran into a reality-TV film crew
huddled in the wind while they waited
for the next bush plane back to available WiFi.
They had a celebrity activist with them who was almost
as famous for championing the wild as for hitting his ex-girlfriend.
As a friend once said, "It's hella' lot easier to love a tree than a person,"
but his wilderness-as-therapy ended in suicide. I talked with the crew for a few
minutes before setting out to follow the ten thousand caribou that were migrating
across the valley as they have for thousands of years, centering the whole ecosystem,
which may stop soon if Exxon drills for oil in their millennial birthing grounds.
Mountains are full of broken people running and climbing and hiking away
from traumas. I'm still waiting to hear back from the famous kayaker
who got excited about removing dams for a hot minute before his
Instagram account went back to hucking waterfalls and drinking
craft beer. But such are the problems of the age, now that
we don't have to outrun world war. Now I can follow
caribou across a mountain range for weeks, alone:
an ancient story, and yet such a modern thing
to do. I can rejoice in seeing no humans.
And what does that say about me?

Our One and Only

Dian Parker

For the past three nights running, Roxanne reveled in the same intoxicating dream. In a world of startling color that sang within a diaphanous landscape, she dove off alizarin and viridian cliffs only to hover, suspended above a dioxazine sea, where human-like frogs and ancient turtles mated amidst cinnabar brain coral the size of elephants.

Today, she went to work as usual. The overheated, crowded bus rattled through the dirty snow. She sweated under her wool coat, had a headache, and felt exhausted, disappointed that yet another breathtaking dream had not become real.

The bus, the snow, and weeks of cold were becoming unbearable. She trudged into the office and didn't say hello to Jeremy, who always had a smile for her. They often walked around the building during lunch, but after three nights of these recent dreams, she couldn't bear to hear any more office gossip. She had six emails from dating services, an update on her college classmates, and a frightening email from the Union of Concerned Scientists. She deleted them all, then burst into tears.

The world was falling apart. Who was she to think she could escape? It was selfish of her to try. She used to pretend she was happy to make other people happy. Now it seemed pointless. Everything that happened in daylight depressed her.

That evening on her way home, she bought a magazine and read about the death of Addwaitya, the 255-year-old tortoise that had been brought to India from the Seychelles islands in the 1700s. Roxanne stared at the photograph of the tortoise for a long time. It looked like the same turtle that had been in her dreams for the past three nights. Had Addwaitya passed through her dream on his way to death?

That night she had another dream—riding underwater on Addwaitya's back. She felt his hard smooth shell against her belly. When she woke in the middle of the night, she lay awake longing to return to Addwaitya, which meant "the one and only" in Sanskrit. She tacked his photograph next to the bed and tried to will herself back into the dream. But she never dreamt of the ancient tortoise, the gigantic coral, or the love-making frog people again.

Roxanne stopped drinking her tap water because it tasted like chlorine and she'd read that chlorine causes your brain to shrink. And if not the chlorine, then fluoride was just as bad. Addwaitya, the 255-year-old tortoise, had died of liver failure, probably from India's water. She started buying bottled water and switched to brushing her teeth with baking soda.

Tuna fish had always been her favorite lunch, but after the afternoon headaches, probably due to the high levels of mercury, she switched to organic avocado and lettuce sandwiches. Jeremy made fun of her "New Age" ways, but she didn't care what he thought. She'd never told him about her dreams, where she lived in her heart of hearts. They were sacred, and besides, Jeremy could never appreciate her pain. She stopped sharing lunch with him.

Her hours at work gradually diminished. She'd leave early, take the filthy, noisy bus back to her apartment, and go straight to bed. And dream.

In one, she was in a large green field. A man walked by holding a bundle of red roses. He laid them on the grass at the feet of a stately woman. Another man walked by with another dozen roses and laid them in another woman's lap. On and on it went, one man with his roses after another. Finally, an older man walked onto the field with a mass of translucent white roses tinged with a blush of pink. He plucked the petals of the rose and tossed them towards Roxanne. She picked up one rose petal and pressed it to her cheek. The petal covered her entire face.

When Roxanne woke up, she felt like her body was melting, like liquid mercury, dripping off the bed. She tried to stay saturated in her dream until her pelvis hurt, pressed into the old, thin mattress. Her pillow was damp with sweat. Cold and shivering, she thought about melting glaciers and poisoned fish. She wouldn't let herself change position. What was the point of comfort? She called in sick to work.

Jeremy knocked on her apartment door three days later. She opened it just enough to stick her face through.

"Oh hi, Jeremy."

"Geeze, Roxie, you look awful. Are you all right?"

"I can't talk now, Jeremy. Don't worry, I'm fine." She locked and bolted the door. From the peephole, she was relieved to see Jeremy walk away. She collapsed onto the couch, thinking how ninety percent of earth's fresh water was in the Antarctic—melting. Polar bears drowning kept flashing across her frontal lobe.

That same night, she dreamt she was lying in the dark next to a man, their shoulders and hips faintly touching. Waves of energy rippled between them. She whispered his name and said, "I am dissolving." He replied, "So am I." She woke, again feeling that her bones were dripping off the bed. She tried to remember the man's face, to no avail.

The next day she dragged herself back to work. All through the day she searched every man's face, even studying Jeremy's. She acted as if nothing had changed, but inside, her bones were floating, unhinged. At lunch, Jeremy tried to take her pulse because he'd studied CPR, but she didn't want anyone to touch her ever again, unless it was the man in her dreams. She was convinced that the man with the plate-sized rose petals was the same man she had melted into. It was only a matter of time.

The next day, Roxanne again left work early. She was sluggish and her eyes itched. March was already too hot. By summer, it would again be unbearable. The sun was too bright—a white hot prediction. Back in the apartment, she turned on her small portable fan, lay down on the couch and put on an eye mask. Her thoughts kept spinning. Carbon dioxide levels were rising, double from 100 years ago. Temperatures will rise between two and ten degrees in five years. Twenty to 400 million tons of grain will be lost to drought.

This time Roxanne dreamt of an endless line of emaciated refugees walking barefoot over baked, cracked soil. Babies hung onto the withered breasts of their mothers. Roxanne woke herself up because she didn't want her dreams to be of the real world. She wanted the paradise world with crystalline water, cool breezes, and thoughtful men. She wanted a world free of pollution. She didn't want her planet to die.

Her mind was again in that torrid zone—insufferable. She was terribly hot. At the corner store, she bought a newspaper and a pint of coffee ice cream. Walking down the street, she read that areas of drought around the globe had more than doubled since 1970. There was a picture of a barefoot Indian woman walking on a dry riverbed. She thought of her dream.

She stopped in the park to rest. Plastic bags floated in the warm breeze that emitted an overwhelming smell of urine. She breathed through her mouth in short gasps and felt claustrophobic. Being outdoors now was as bad as at work, where all that recycled stale air circled endlessly through the cubicles. There was always someone coughing. She'd have to wear a mask, outdoors and inside, wherever she went. She practiced keeping her eyes cast down, as if hidden.

Next to the bench where she sat were the remains of a huge maple tree. It had been cut down because people in town thought it was too dangerous in the wind. She'd read that one deciduous tree could remove 50 pounds of carbon from the air per year. She looked at the old tree stump and burst into tears.

"Are you all right?"

Thinking she was dreaming, she didn't bother to move her mouth. *Because the earth is dying.*

A man sat down next to her on the park bench. "What's that you said?"

Was she dreaming?

"Why are you crying?"

Was she crying? He wore the same green sweatshirt he had on when he was throwing the rose petals.

"Did you know that Category 5 hurricanes have doubled in the last 35 years?" she said.

"No, I didn't know that. That's really alarming."

"You really think so?"

"Think what?"

"That it's really alarming?"

"Why, of course I do. Who wouldn't?"

She whispered, "Lots of people."

She thought about her dream of melting while lying next to him and burst out laughing. She felt a surge of air rush down her throat. In the next moment, she felt lightheaded and leaned slightly into him. He smelled like the pitch of a pine tree. He leaned back, barely brushing her shoulder. She daren't move.

They sat like this for a long time until it grew dark, and her ice cream lay untouched. She remembered and offered him some. His eyes were the palest blue; she was reminded of her first paradise dream. Things were coming together so fast!

"Ice cream? It's not that hot!"

She felt hurt and ate a spoonful, looking away.

"I'm sorry," he said.

And then it all came rushing out. About the maple tree's death and the turtle's death. The whole planet dying. She told him about the bad air and the mercury, about the islands of plastic in the ocean and the drowning polar bears, about all the sick chickens being slaughtered only because people crammed thousands of them together forcing them to lay. "Oh, what are we to do if there's no home left for any of us?" she cried out. He took her hand and softly stroked it. She watched his long fingers feather across her palm. Her hardened core was melting rapidly.

She moved into his house three months later. He lived in a two-story stone house with a porch and a basement. She loved to go down there when it was hot, sit on the cool cement floor, and eat her ice cream.

Sometimes when he wasn't working, he'd come and sit with her. They'd make up stories about how the world was vibrant and healthy with lots of good clean water to drink for everyone.

She knew it wasn't so and finally stopped pretending.

"Listen, Roxanne, you've got to stop taking this so hard. Yes, it is horrible but what can we do, my sweet?"

"We've got to *feel,* John. *Feel.*"

"But I do feel. I feel anger and despair."

"No, I mean feel what the planet must feel. Not our kind of feelings. No, not them. But the earth's feelings, the bear's feelings, the turtle's feelings. Their feelings."

"But I don't know what those feelings are, Roxanne."

"Tonight I'll show you."

That night, with John lying close, their arms and legs touching just like in her melting dream, she said, "Now concentrate on your chest. Feel how much you love me."

John loved Roxanne. Truly. And it was always so peaceful lying next to her, listening to her sweet, low whisper. Soon he fell asleep. Roxanne too fell asleep, wrapped in his arms.

In her dream, she saw a lizard, gazelle, an ibex, and a moose, all standing on a tiny island in the middle of the sea. The island got smaller and smaller as the ocean swelled, lapping at the receding shore. The animals moved closer together until they stood huddled on one tiny piece of land out in the middle of the vast sea. A piece of bleached plastic drifted by. The animals began to panic.

She made herself wake up. She shook John awake. "We haven't much time," she said.

"What happened?" he asked with concern.

"You'll see. Maybe tonight."

Every night thereafter John lay close beside Roxanne so he too could feel the earth. Maybe if he could feel as intensely as she did, together they could do something. She asked him to try and find her hand in his dreams and grab hold tight, then she could take him into her dream. He had only to look for her hand. And never let go.

One night he found it. Her beautiful black hand shone in the darkness like a beacon of light. John reached as far as he could, but her hand floated away into the void. He woke up feeling afraid. When he told Roxanne, she was ecstatic.

"Soon, John. Soon."

Night after night they lay side by side holding hands, willing themselves to find each other in their dreams. Sometimes John doubted the point of dreaming together, but then Roxanne would show him yet another scientific article of another plant, animal, or insect extinction that the government was trying to silence. A report of the series of seventeen tornados in two days where there had never been tornados before. The death of the last remaining coral in the Great Barrier Reef.

The night after Hurricane Emanuel ripped away Florida from its neighboring states, John saw Roxanne's hand in his dream. She was floating above him. She reached out her hand. He lunged forward and caught it.

She led him into the ocean to the very bottom, far, far below. Still holding onto his hand, Roxanne wrapped her naked legs around his waist, pressing her forehead against his. Then she pushed him away, into the arms of a giant octopus, five times larger than his body. The creature reached out and wrapped its tentacles around John's naked body. John felt the countless suction cups gripping his skin. But the most startling thing of all was its eye. It looked alien, all-knowing. The eye was looking at John as if it knew him. Like it had birthed him. John felt himself sinking deeper. When he hit bottom, the jolt woke him up.

He was in bed, with Roxanne wrapped around his body. Her arms were tangled around his head, her hair draped across his face; her legs wrapped round his waist so tightly that he found it hard to breathe.

"Roxanne!"

When she didn't respond and remained cemented to him, he began to panic. He tried to kick away her legs and pry her fingers loose from his hair. He pleaded with Roxanne to let go. It seemed as if he hadn't breathed for a very long time, felt like he was still under water, that he might die. Maybe this was his time.

He decided to stop fighting and let go.

When Roxanne felt John surrender, she unwrapped herself from his body. She stroked his face, whispering, "Shhh…" He began to relax, letting his body sink into the bed, but then recalled the giant octopus at the bottom of the ocean. He felt suffocated.

"Yes, you see, John? You see now, don't you? It is the same for them. They are losing their home, and they don't understand. All the creatures are panicking. I am panicking. Now you are panicking too."

During the following weeks, John and Roxanne tried out many ideas to quell their panic. They had to do something, take action. They recycled, put a compost bin in their back yard, installed two solar panels, and unhooked from the power grid. They rode bicycles. They changed to energy-saving light bulbs. They unplugged their refrigerator and used a cooler instead. Roxanne stopped eating ice cream. They wrote letters to congressmen, went to protest marches, signed petitions, called senators. Was any of this making a difference? They didn't know.

Still, John was beginning to *feel* the earth's distress and that gave Roxanne hope. Finally, there was someone who understood. But the more John became proficient in dreaming with Roxanne, the more depressed he became.

After she led him in a dream to a massive coral reef coated with oil, he told her he couldn't sleep with her anymore. "I just can't keep doing this, Roxanne. I'm exhausted all the time. It feels like *I'm* dying." What he didn't say was if he had one more sick planet dream, he might have to ask her to move out.

So they slept in separate rooms. Freed from having to take John with her, Roxanne's dreams left the earth and began flying to other planets—healthy, thriving planets with their inhabitants busy being happy and kind. Every night she played and laughed with them. And every day she went to a job where she felt depleted, lifeless. After weeks of deliberating, she finally quit her job.

She spent the afternoons lying in the back yard, waiting for the earth to tell her what to do. She felt that she and the planet were both on the verge of a tipping point.

John convinced Roxanne to take a break, go away for a while. She rented a tiny cabin on a peninsula. She saw from the map it was surrounded by state forest and three miles from a national park. She saw the swath of green on the map and wanted to be tucked deep into the trees, if there were any left. She would find out what to do. John kissed her goodbye and said, "Try to be easy on yourself, Roxanne, but do whatever it takes. Come back to me beaming."

On the bus ride to the cabin, Roxanne watched out her window mile after mile after mile of clear-cut forest. The gray stumps and the building-high slash piles of burning branches, along with lumbering logging trucks stacked high with fresh trees, was too much. She put on her eye mask. When the driver called out, "Your place, miss!" she stumbled out of the bus and staggered into the office to register. Without looking around, she ran to her cabin, threw herself face down on the bed, and wept. Now she knew what raping the forest meant.

The trucks came and went every day, all day. She heard them from her cabin bed. The windows shook. When she was brave enough to venture outdoors, she saw more huge trees hanging over the back of the trucks. She asked the woman at the check-in desk where all the logs were going.

"Japan. That's how we all survive around here," she said and went about her business.

"Fifty pounds of carbon will no longer be absorbed by each of those trees per year," Roxanne muttered as she trudged back to the cabin.

On the third day in the cabin, she ventured far enough into the woods to get away from the sounds of logging. There were a few stately cedars and different varieties of pine trees she'd never experienced before. She breathed the cool air and smelled the moist humus of the earth. She lay on the soft pine needles and dreamt of John and woke up laughing. She felt better than she had in a long time. The air was perfect. She had lost the sensation of suffocation. She saw a deer peeking out behind an old growth cedar.

Each day Roxanne walked deeper into the damp, mossy woods, feeling the soft, spongy earth under her feet and taking in deep draughts of crystalline air. Everything green nestled in rich chocolate brown. It was so still that she thought she could feel the earth breathing. "You are alive!" she laughed. She saw chipmunks, squirrels, deer, a raccoon, an opossum, and heard the trilling of birds. She measured the girth of an old-growth cedar tree with her outstretched arm. Four lengths. But maybe all of this was only a dream, a mere memory of what once was. Realities were braiding in her mind. She didn't know anymore what was real.

One day, Roxanne walked east through the forest. After only a few brief minutes, she came to another clear-cut. One moment she was cool, in lovely, sweet dampness, and the next moment the air was hot, dry, and brittle. The ground was hard and cracked. Huge stumps littered the landscape as far as she could see, with a few thin, bent-over trees left struggling in the wind. Only the weak were left, along with piles of garbage: fiberglass insulation, truck tires, blue plastic, tin cans, meth lab debris. The soil was gray, bleached out.

Roxanne lay down and stared up through the few spindly pine branches that were left. She lay still, trying to feel the earth. It was quiet. The earth felt stunned, like after a fierce battle that had been fought and lost. The dead and wounded were strewn all around as far as she could see, but she couldn't hear any moans of pain or final death throes. She thought, *this was an all-out surrender. Nature did not resist.* Roxanne saw smoke from the heaps of branches and stumps smoldering after the rain. *The stench of war.* She wondered what the trees felt, standing in one place for hundreds of years, stretching upwards, reaching for the sun. They had provided homes for owl, eagle, squirrel, jay, fox, deer, insects, fungi, algae.

She had to stop. There were too many creatures to count. All gone. All gone.

That night, Roxanne left the cabin and walked barefoot back into the forest. She wanted to feel the earth, to feel the trees at night. In the precious darkness, things happened that weren't allowed in the light. Night held mystery and without mystery all was hopeless. Nature was a great mystery and that was what Roxanne longed for, like her dreams. In daylight the world had gone bad. In daylight Roxanne saw the clear-cuts. She saw the stagnant water rimmed with rust and the filthy piles of rubbish. At night the devastation was hidden from view. Her witness body could relax.

The next day she walked towards the sound of chainsaws. In the distance she saw a logger sitting on the sideboard of a truck, eating lunch. That evening she saw the same logging truck with eleven massive logs stacked on the back. She could kill that logger just like he'd killed every tree. But it would solve nothing.

She had to change his mind.

Every day, for three days, she brought him a sandwich and a cup of coffee. He did most of the talking during these lunch hours, while she looked carefully into his eyes and listened to the sound of his voice. The logger talked about his four kids and bragged especially about his six-year-old son. "The little lad is strong. No fear that I can see." She watched as he unconsciously placed his hand over his heart when he said, "the little lad."

Roxanne told the man that she was writing an article for her local paper about loggers and logging practices. When she asked about clear-cutting, he said, "It's called harvesting timber. The trees are crops and need to be harvested. Cuts down on wildfires, removes insect pests, diseases. Opens up the forest real good. Doug Fir and the Southern Pine like full sun, so we're doing them a favor. And we always leave a buffer along the side of the road. A beauty strip." While he talked, Roxanne watched his hands speak and his shoulders lift and sag. She memorized what she could.

Every night after she'd been with the logger, she lay on the wet earth behind her cabin. First, she'd stare at the stars and their vast magnitude. When her mind started to spin like a galaxy, she'd close her eyes and zero in on the logger's face. See his red cheeks and dark circles under his dark brown eyes, the bushy eyebrows beginning to gray, and his red plaid hat, cocked slightly to the right. She imagined him walking through dense forest holding onto his son's hand.

Falling asleep, Roxanne dreamt of endless forests of old growth trees. In the distance she could see the logger and his son, walking through the woods. In the next night's dream, his son was an adult and the trees even larger. Every night she worked on the logger in her dreams.

The day she was to leave on the bus she gave him her address so he could send her a photograph of his son. They shook hands. Roxanne memorized the calluses on his palm and the stub where his pinky finger used to be.

When she returned home, John saw there was color in her cheeks and she seemed more relaxed. Roxanne told him about the clear-cuts and the logger, and took great care in describing him to John, so they could add him to their dreams.

That night he slept with her, and every night after. Sometimes they dreamed together, walking through dark, fecund forests that stretched unbroken for hundreds of miles. Thick dripping moss and rushing brooks of pure, drinkable water. Insects whirred, birds sang, and animals gamboled. Unafraid.

Two months after she'd been to the cabin on the peninsula, Roxanne received a postcard from the logger. On the back was a child's scrawled drawing of a huge tree with a man and a boy standing on the top branches waving their hands. Underneath it said: "I quit logging. I've started a tree nursery and my son is a great little helper. Gary and Wendell."

Now, if she could only dream 24 hours a day. There was so much work to be done.

Out in the Woods

Bret Serbin

Driving down the Forest Service road, it was impossible not to think about the murder.

Kylen Schulte and Crystal Turner practically sat with us in my SUV, even though the bodies of the newlyweds had been discovered at a campsite a few weeks earlier. Schulte, like us, hailed from Montana, and we both knew all too well how rare it is to find fellow queer women in the Big Sky State. It's rarer, of course, to fall prey to random violence on a camping trip. But for girls like us, it isn't unheard of.

In fact, my partner for the trip had to ask which murder I was talking about when I inevitably brought it up. Was I referring to Rebecca Wight, who was shot to death on the Appalachian Trail by a man who watched her get intimate with her girlfriend, Claudia Brenner? Or did I mean Julianne Williams and Laura Winans, a couple that was found bound and gagged in Shenandoah National Park? None of the above. The murder in question took place in Moab, that outdoor desert haven, after the two women described feeling creeped out by another camper near their tent.

As we snaked deeper into the forest, we debated the appearance of queerness.

No one would suspect something just by looking at us, I argued. A same-sex couple couldn't be top of mind for the residents in the few houses we glimpsed through the trees. My partner wasn't so sure.

She pointed out my undercut, and mentioned how glad she was that we hadn't taken her Subaru. We checked a second time to make sure our emergency contact knew our location.

When the road began to climb above the trees, we paused to look out at the valley below us. Clouds crept in over the Selkirk Mountains, shading the landscape in a moody blue and gray. We had booked a stay in a fire tower lookout in the hopes of watching an incredible sunset. But as evening drew closer, there was no sun in sight. Nor was there a soul, until we looked away from the vista, back to the dirt road, where a black Jeep had quietly pulled into our path. The vehicle sat ever-so-slightly towards the cliff edge, leaving just enough space on the inside of the road for my Honda to slither past.

My partner and I tried to look into the approaching cab as I eased us forward, but the windows were tinted beyond any hope of transparency. I felt like I was passing through the jaws of a grizzly for the perilous second that our vehicles lined up next to each other. My passenger clutched a can of bear spray. Then we were through, winding further up the hill, trying to exhale our relief as we both, without acknowledging it, monitored the rearview mirror.

At the base of the tower, we grabbed at any hint of security we could find. There was freshly charred detritus in a few fire rings, I pointed out. My companion wasn't satisfied. The people who had built those fires might not be friendly. Trails branched off from the gravel circle just below the tower, she noted. At this, it was my turn at contrarian. We'd get no warning if an approaching hiker crept up one of the trails to our camp. We both looked uneasily at the lonely wooden outhouse nestled in a field of weeds a few hundred feet from the base of the tower and thought with mounting dread about venturing to use the facility in the middle of the approaching night. The clouds moved in closer as we contemplated our surroundings.

Both full of misgivings, we grabbed our bags from my car and started up the forty feet to our cabin in the clouds. The car and the outhouse shrunk from view as we ascended. We lost our bearings on the location of the trail crossings. My friend asked what my plan would be to escape the rickety tower if an attacker showed up. Then she stopped. We both looked in horror to see the gate swinging open in the breeze, which was blowing harder and harder as the storm we had spotted began to settle on our mountain.

I had no doubt the rangers had warned us the gate would be locked before our arrival. I had made sure to secure the combination to undo the lock before we lost cell phone service. There was no reason the gate should have been left to gape at us.

My friend immediately raised her voice. "The boys said they were just ten minutes behind us, right?" she called out like a good actor pretending to be a bad actor in a comedy. I silently pulled my bear spray from my water bottle pouch and followed as she crept up the last set of wooden steps. Our movements were robotic, our breath suspended in our chests, our ostentatious conversation nonsensical. We climbed the wooden steps and rounded the blind corner, bracing to put the plan we had just discussed into action. Finally, forty feet in the air, we found ourselves alone.

That night, in the tower, we jumped with each flash of lightning. Night fell without the hoped-for sunset, wrapping us in a cloud as black as the Jeep from that afternoon. With it came the storm, whipping raindrops at the 360-degree windows that formed our only shelter.

Lightning struck out practically at eye level, while thunderclaps and gusts of wind rattled our precarious home for the night. Elevated forty feet up in the air on top of a mountain, my friend complained that she felt claustrophobic.

"We're way more likely to get into trouble in an urban area than here," I said, after I reminded her for the tenth time where I had set the bear spray.

"Yeah, but the way we'd be murdered here would be worse," she contended unhelpfully.

We decided to occupy ourselves by reading the logbook from previous visitors. We divided up the entries, working by headlamp to make out the handwriting. One of mine described the place as "spooky." In hers, my friend read about a pack rat that rummaged through the place. I came across a woman who described waking up in the middle of the night to a sound she couldn't place, only to discover it was her sister in the next cot.

We put away the logbook and tried to play cards. My partner explained the rules of the game, and we giggled nervously with each hand. I attempted to snap a photo of her at the wooden table, only to find unnerving shadows in the windowpanes behind her when I looked back at the image. We checked the time, tried not to, and talked about nothing. Without warning, our flimsy door shot open.

I don't remember if I was the only one who jumped, nor do I recall which one of us blamed the sudden movement on the wind. There was no one in the doorway, no shadowy figure illuminated by the lightning, no sound of footsteps in the stillness after the thunder. But we had our bags packed in an instant.

I threw my sleeping bag down the stairs. My friend left behind the water jugs we had purchased at a gas station just hours before. We barely remembered to lock the gate behind us—perhaps a little like the visitors who had come the night before.

We hurled our belongings into our car, all of the tension from the day unleashed in a flurry of panic. I tossed the keys into the front seat as the rain pelted us, then watched with shock as my friend threw the front door shut. "Don't close it!" I cried as it clicked.

I dove for the handle just in time to avoid the automatic lock, relieved as the headlights cut a tiny, eerie circle in the darkness in front of us. We crept back down the winding forest road, neither of us daring to voice our fear that we might see the Jeep again. My soaked sandal squeaked on the brake pedal, and I debated internally whether I would take the shoes off if I had to make a dash into the trees.

When we arrived back at a ghost town we had passed—the site where a school and dozens of houses had burned down years before—my flummoxed friend struggled to make sense of the map. I refused to slow down, finally recognizing at the last second a bridge we had passed earlier in the day. And with that, we were back on pavement, where we let ourselves believe we were safe.

When will we awaken
to all that connects us?

© 2022 by Andie Thrams

Between Trees

Sarah Scruggs

    Descending down the red clay hills,
heart hurting, head pounding,
Footsteps and tears falling.
All of my reasons for seeking the wild:
    Breakups,
loss of friends,
relatives transitioned to ancestors—
coming Out only to be shut down.
    Another headline:
Unarmed Black Man Killed in Routine Traffic Stop.
Irreversible damage:
Glacier National Park May Lose Glaciers By 2030.
    Hopelessness sounds off with the birdsong.
Blame sneaks into the fill of my jacket.
Regret sticks to the soles of my boots.
A deep hurt lingers with the clouds overhead.

    Still the outside air fills me.
The distance from my starting point awards time to think.
The stars at night comfort me, reminding me they never left.
The new day brings a renewed mindset.
    Miles pass and the pain slowly releases its grip.
The sun shines on my face and warms the fire within.
Grasses rustle with the wind and tell me of my strength.
The brush arbor hangs overhead, strokes my hair, says it'll be okay.
    Emerging, I'm reminded of my ancestors
how they were hurt and healed,
overwhelmed and overcame.
I march on with them.

Zone 28

Frank Haberle

Do you remember the bus ride into Denali?

It was the backpacker bus, I think, and we were the only backpackers going in deep that day. We sat in silence right behind the driver, an old woman with long white hair flowing down around her park ranger jacket and dream-catcher earrings. I stared out my window at the haze of glacial creeks winding their way through the chrome-green brush, and you were silently sewing a patch onto a hole in your sleeping bag.

I was real hungover. I remember that the guy we hitched a ride with the night before kept feeding me beers—they just kept coming—and I sensed you were pissed off about it. You thought I had slipped on a one-night bender; in truth I had bent, and fully broke, some months before.

I remember how the bus came around a bend, and the sun burst through the clouds. "Look at that!" the driver yelled. She caught my eye in the rearview mirror and pointed ahead, across a sweep of metallic tundra and silver waters draining into the horizon. The Great Range and its jagged foothills, draped in cloud for the past month, were suddenly visible in the distance. Denali, a huge white mass, filled half the sky. I focused on it, and all the beer and alcohol from the prior night, and the previous nights, flushed through my blood stream.

"Sweet Jesus," I think I said.

"It's just a mountain," I remember you said, pulling needle through nylon.

"I hope the sky opens up when we're in there," I said. "I hope we see it up close."

You shrugged, not looking up. The clouds quickly sealed themselves around the summit, many miles away and far from where we were going. The hangover poured itself back into me. But in time, I knew, it would evaporate. Three or four days out in the backcountry, and it would be gone.

The driver pulled over on a bridge. She pulled a lever, and the bus door exhaled.

"Here you go," she said. "Zone 28, right up there to the left."

"Where?" you asked her.

"You're headed right up there someplace." The driver pointed to a raging torrent of green water. It was ripping a gap between two steep ledges. "That's the pass. You just need to stay on the left side of that gorge. And the right side of the next gorge."

"But I don't see a trail," you said.

The driver turned around and looked at you like you were crazy.

"There are no trails anywhere, sweetie," the driver said to you. "This is Denali."

"Well, thanks for the lift!" I said, climbing down.

"You can go back and stay in the registered campsites, you know. They let you do day hikes without a permit. You don't have to stay out here."

"Thanks," you said.

"Yeah, but don't go trying to sneak into another zone. Park Service catches you in another zone without a permit, you're out two hundred bucks. And try to stay up high," the driver continued. "Look for the goat paths. When you hit the far side of this ridge, there's a valley. The valley's amazing. Good luck to yah. They gave you a bear cannister?"

"Yep!" I said, pulling my pack on. It was cold and damp there, the creek below the bridge funneling through an unseen gorge, someplace where we were going. And I was sweating, I remember—already sweating out the night before, the week before, the month before.

"And make a lot of noise," the driver said. "There's a lot of traffic up there this time of year."

"Traffic?" you asked. Then the bus door closed, and the driver pulled away.

Do you remember how impossibly hard it was to hike there?

From the road it all looked like a shiny carpet, a treeless lunar landscape. But when you started uphill, it was a tangled maze of intertwined vines and branches, six feet high, and your boots sunk into spongy undergrowth. At first it was okay—we climbed down off the bridge and followed a sandbar along the surging gray water. Then the sandbar gave way to the water. We climbed up onto a parallel ledge that followed the water, but then that crumbled back into the water. We had to work our way up the steep hillside. I pushed into a wall of stubbled green plants. They were a foot over my head, and pushed me back. I pushed harder, and they gave way. Soon I was pulling myself up a steep, slick incline through twisted shoots, yelling for bears. We had to drag our backpacks through the tangled mess behind us.

After a long climb up, we broke into something like a sloping meadow, where the brush was only waist-deep. Every so often we came across a depression in the plants where something large and heavy was rolling around fairly recently. We could see the park road, now a brown strip down far below us. The creek hissed somewhere below us in the notch now forming to our right. Sparkling silver clouds rotated just feet above our heads, brushing against the rocky red peaks poking up to the left, to the right.

"Do you have any idea where we're going?" you asked.

"Just west, and north," I said. "We follow the gorge to our right. We break over this ridge, then the next one, and after that there's a valley. It's supposed to be unbelievably beautiful. We can camp up above the valley."

"This doesn't seem very passable," you said. "There's no trail."

"I think we just follow the gorge," I said. "If we stay up here, we can't miss it."

I looked around. The glaciers of the higher mountains, somewhere just over the next ridge, were emitting that eerie, phosphorous light. I was starting to feel the shakes kick in, bad. Chronic remorse sunk into my thoughts. *What did I say last night? Was I an asshole? Did you think I was an asshole?* Under normal circumstances I'd just find a bar and have a few beers, to steady me, to smooth everything out. But we were five miles into a major Denali bushwhack, and there were no bars in sight. I didn't want you to see how bad I was shaking. So I just started talking.

"Yeah, so I read someplace that the mountains out here are so big that they generate their own weather," I remember saying. "The climate change is so severe from the ocean, up the steep slopes and around all these deep glaciers and ice, and it all creates these huge columns of vapor. So it's like this huge block of energy, all jutting out into the ocean."

"Wow," you said. You were squinting up at the sky. The swirl of silver clouds, as we stood there, suddenly became menacing.

"Yeah, and these storms come up through the gulf, these huge storms, and they wrap around the mountains. And before you know it, they're just spinning around it in circles, just spinning. For days and days. Like this rain here. This rainstorm." I held out my hands as big, cold, driven drops splashed against them. "This rainstorm was probably here last night. And will probably be here again tomorrow morning."

"That's great." You pulled your poncho on.

"That's unless, of course, one of these serious numbers come along. I think the soldiers back in the war called it the 'Yukon Express.' A really huge thing, really high up, a high-pressure thing. They come in from way down at the end of the Peninsula or someplace, and they push down onto these storms. And then it's like, you know, all bets are off. Summer blizzards. Serious wind disturbances, wind storms. Really powerful stuff." The rain started driving down harder. "I don't know. I know it sounds really stupid." I gave up.

"I think it is really powerful, what you just said."

"Really?"

"Really. It's all about energy. It's all this energy up here."

I looked at you, but you were looking up at the sky. Streaks of mud, leaves and vines were tangled in your hair and streaked down your face, but your eyes were shining. I pulled my anorak around me, but I was already soaked.

"Well, I guess we should get moving again," I said.

Do you remember how we pushed farther up the ledges for hours?

We clawed through the brush. We crossed steep mudslides dropping down into the gorge. On a high point we spotted a clear ledge jutting out over the gorge and climbed down to it. It was a fully exposed shoulder of polished rock, ten feet wide and twenty feet long, dropping steeply on either side down into the gorge, several hundred feet below. From the ledge we could clearly see that there was no beautiful valley anywhere in our near future, that there was another, steeper ridge across to the north and west of us. The sides of the gorge were steep and filled with deep brush; there was no clear way to climb down the banks. But for the moment, the rain stopped and early evening sunlight crept into the gorge. A beautiful, clear creek bubbled icy fresh water just a few yards downhill. We set up the tent, tying the fly lines off on large flat rocks, because we couldn't dig the spikes into the rock, and the soft spots were too soft. We hung our soaked raingear to dry on the lines.

I remember what we had for dinner that night. We boiled noodles on your camping stove. You were staring up at the stark ridges above us, across from us.

"Do you really think this is a safe spot?"

"I think a bear would have a hell of a time climbing up here, if that's what you mean," I said.

"It's not just the bears," you said. "It's just so...isolated. We're just cut off from everything here."

We ate in silence. I started to feel better. The first round of the shakes was wearing off, and the prospect of no access to alcohol for a few nights in the wilderness started to feel manageable. After dinner I climbed up through the brush to hide our food cannister a safe distance from the tent. In the brush below me I came across the bleached skull of a ram, its horns perfectly intact, lying face down in the grass.

"Hey," I yelled back to you. "You gotta check this out."

You walked up, looked, and turned away.

"Why did you need to show me that?" you asked, walking back down to the tent.

"I don't know, I've just never seen anything like it," I said. In the still evening air, I stared down into the skull for a long time. The eye sockets, though inverted, stared back at me. Suddenly, I was consumed with thirst. I took the cannister a little farther up the hill, then climbed down to stick my head in the icy creek for as long as I could hold it there. The wind was starting to pick up again, increasingly, in bursts across the shimmering brush. The last light faded from the gorge. You were sitting on a large rock by the stove boiling water for tea, shielding the flame from the pressing, searching wind. I sat down on the rock across from you.

"I'm sorry about the skull. I sort of thought it was interesting."

"Can I ask you something?"

"Sure."

"Why are you drinking again?"

"Because I'm thirsty."

"I don't mean the water."

"Me either."

"I'm serious."

"Me too."

"Can you try to stop? For good?"

"Unless there's a bar under this rock, I'm stopped at the moment."

"No, like, when we get back to civilization? And wherever we go after that?"

I tried to think of how many hours it would be. We were planning to be out here for three or four days, but we hadn't really discussed what would happen after that.

"I can absolutely try."

"It's just that you're a totally different person when you're not drinking. It's like you're here. Totally. Whatever 'here' is."

"Okay."

"Before I came up here to meet you, when you called me from the road, you told me you were sober, like, three times. Were you really sober?"

"I was trying to be. I guess maybe I wasn't."

"Can you try now?"

"I'll try."

"Can you promise?"

"Sure," I remember saying. I tried to make it sound like this promise wasn't a big deal, but I knew myself better than that, and I think you did too. By making that promise, a clock was set. Our time together, way up here or back down there, would be brief. "I'll give it a go."

Do you remember the terrible wind?

We were sitting on logs, sheltered by the overhanging brush drinking tea while the wind continued to pick up. The wind blew downward, pressing the damp, clinging brush down against us. Plants and leaves and debris started sailing over our heads. My rain cover flipped off the line and flew straight up the gorge like a torn parachute. We gathered the rest of the raingear and crawled into the tent. The wind kept blowing, increasing in intensity. By midnight the tent was shuddering, the fly flapping so loudly it was screaming, the tent poles bending down all around us.

"Do you think we're going to get blown off the ledge?" you yelled, lying next to me in your sleeping bag.

"I think it's definitely possible," I yelled back.

"Is there anything we can do?"

"I don't think so. Just wait it out I guess."

Something rattled away down the ledge, probably one of the rocks we used to tie down the tent. The roar of the flapping grew louder. The tent bent down further around us.

"I think you're finally starting to wear me down," I remember you yelled. "I think you can put your arm around me now."

Do you remember when, at last, the terrible wind stopped?

It was later that night, and the roaring air suddenly stilled itself. Wide awake, I heard it hurtle up the slopes of the mountains through the gorge and then disappear into that valley, the one we never reached. Exhausted, I fell into a deep sleep. And I remember, to this day, that long after the wind had passed through, I kept my arm around you—and you kept yours around mine—like we were still trying to hold each other down.

Drinking Tea on Black Elk Peak

Nicholas Trandahl

*"Then I was standing on the highest mountain of them all,
and round about beneath me was the whole hoop of the world."*
-Nicholas Black Elk, Lakota visionary

Snow on the mountaintop
and a cold wind whipping
Lakota prayer flags—
ribbons of color.

Huddling against stone
to stay out of the wind,
I sip from a thermos
of hot rooibos—
gaze with wonder
at what wintry wind
does to reverence,
carrying it far over the mountains
and east, toward dawn's yellow bloom
over the Badlands—
toward the holy fires rising
like a Sun Dance.

Steam from the tea
curls into the frigid air
like smoke from burning sage.
I can almost hear voices
crying out in song.

Summit Storm

Steve Gardiner

We had climbed the east side of Mount Rainier and reached the crater rim, when a late-spring storm, hiding behind the mountain on the west side, released its rage on us. Within minutes we were staggering in a blizzard as we left the 14,410-foot summit, the highest point in the state of Washington.

There had been small flurries of snow throughout the morning, but nothing indicating the fierce nature of the storm that threatened our descent. We had placed wands, small stakes with orange flags like the ones used by surveyors at a construction site, in the snow on the way up in case a storm did occur. That preparation was critical as we faced the blinding conditions.

It had taken over eight hours to climb the mountain from the stone hut at Camp Muir. The descent should take less time, but with visibility so limited, we were all concerned. We had tied ourselves together as three rope teams. Bill Johnson, who had climbed Rainier before, was leading us down. He moved slowly, searching in the storm for each orange wand. Bonnie Plant, on her first climb, was behind him, and I was last on the lead rope. The two other rope teams followed closely behind, keeping us united as a team.

As Bill searched for each wand, I stood at the previous one. If we had trouble finding the next wand, at least we would know where the route was and could return to that wand and begin the search again. The system was slow, but safe.

Bill yelled each time he found a wand, and I moved down to him. We repeated this search process several times, descending some 800 feet from the top. The snow increased, and I struggled to see Bill ahead of me. Finally, he moved far enough ahead that I could not see him at all. I watched Bonnie walk, using her progress as an indication of where Bill was and how he was doing.

I stood next to a wand and watched Bonnie move slowly. She turned slightly to her left, then her body jerked forward. She fell headfirst down the mountain. Bill had walked off a snowy embankment and fallen, not a free fall, but he was sliding quickly. As he slid, the rope tightened between him and Bonnie, pulling her off her feet.

When she fell, I turned toward the slope of the mountain and sprawled face down, driving my ice axe deep into the snow, a move climbers call a self-arrest. I put my body weight on the axe and in a second, felt the tug as the weight of Bill and Bonnie stretched the rope tied to the waist of my seat harness.

Behind me, on the second rope, Kirk Johnson, Bill's son, quickly sat on my back, helping to anchor me to the mountain. Then he, Mark Brackin and Norm Pedersen pulled on the rope to help Bonnie and Bill regain their positions and climb back up.

There were several tense minutes, but soon Bonnie and Bill were beside us. The seven of us stood together, feeling very small on the side of the massive mountain. The storm was a complete whiteout. The sky and mountain had become one.

It was a short conversation. We could not continue down. If we did, the next slip could be far more serious. We would have to dig in.

We fell to the snow, scraping with our ice axes. We had to get inside the mountain. I chopped the frozen slope, tossing the loose chunks. We could neither hear nor see them as they dropped. What an irony. The same substance which threatened to take our lives was the very thing we hoped would save us.

While the ice axes are sharp, they are narrow, not particularly efficient for carving caves large enough for seven people. I hacked at the snow and dug down vertically to make a flat face. Then I slashed horizontally back into the mountain. The snow was hardpacked, pounded by weeks of wintry winds. With each stroke of the axe, the snow broke off in blocks. As the horizontal hole expanded, I lay on my side, swinging the axe overhead, breaking out more blocks. I pushed them outward toward my feet and kicked them out the door of the developing shelter.

I rolled from side to side, chopping with both arms. At one point, I stopped, my arms aching from the strain. I thought about how sore my arms would be the next day, but then realized that if we didn't get everyone inside, we might not be around the next day to feel the soreness. I chopped harder. Soon I had my whole body inside and could now stop going deeper into the mountain and could just expand the room I had already created. Others were working on two more caves nearby.

In less than two hours, we had created three small holes and could get all seven of us inside, out of the wind, and in the relative comfort and warmth of the snow caves. Outside, the temperature had dropped below zero, and the wind was fifty miles per hour. Inside it was calm and quiet. At 13,600 feet elevation, we settled in, not knowing how long we might be there. It was a strong storm. It might last an hour, or it might last much longer. We could only wait.

And hope.

The first time the snow threatened me was on a much shorter trip—only sixty miles through western Nebraska. I had been student teaching in Scottsbluff and driving to Alliance on the weekends to stay with my parents and visit friends. On one Friday afternoon, a storm was approaching, but I was sure I had time to get to Alliance before it hit.

The road report on the radio even confirmed my belief. "A winter storm should drop several inches of snow on the Nebraska Panhandle tonight. As of three o'clock, the roads between Scottsbluff and Torrington, Wyoming, are clear with some drifting snow. Highway 385 between Scottsbluff and Alliance is clear. Highway 2 between Scottsbluff and Ogallala is..."

I drove east on Highway 2. A few snowflakes swayed along the asphalt. My radio played the top hits for the week. At the junction of Highway 385, I turned north, and quickly noticed the change in weather. The telephone poles beside the road grew faint, then disappeared. My little Ford Maverick shied into the ditch, then came to a halt, sinking deep into the snow.

It would not move forward or backward. I slid out the door and opened the trunk, grabbing a few extra shirts and a coat. I got back inside the car and put on the clothing. I didn't know what I should do, what I could do.

People die in blizzards.

I sat there for several minutes. I could see a farmhouse just down the road during the brief breaks in the storm. "I'll walk on the edge of the road. That way I can follow it back to the car," I said, trying to reassure myself.

I pushed at the car door, but it would not open. The wind was stronger now. I leaned my shoulder against the door, pressing with all my strength. The weight of the wind drove the door against my chest as I squeezed out.

Stumbling along the shoulder of the road, I got enough glimpses of the house to keep walking. At the driveway I turned, climbed across the wooden gate, and approached the house.

"Oh, no! It's abandoned!"

I looked quickly back. My car was gone from sight. Slowly, I walked back to the roadway. At the edge, I turned, the wind blowing me from behind, as if ushering me back to my car. I stayed along the edge of the road, knowing that I would soon meet my car. I thought I was getting close when I saw a flashing yellow light. A snow plow.

"Are you alright?" the driver asked.

"Yes," I shouted. "Where are you going?"

"I'm turning around and going back to Scottsbluff," he replied. "Can I give you a ride?"

I pulled myself up into the cab. He drove me back to my apartment, as I explained my story and, from time to time, removed another shirt.

As soon as I was inside my apartment, I crawled in bed, still shivering from the experience. I couldn't believe what had happened. My car was in a ditch, and I would have to figure out some way to retrieve it once the storm ended.

The phone rang. It was my mother. I hadn't thought to tell anyone else about my experience, so my mom learned about it from a highway patrolman who saw my abandoned car, looked up the license plate, and called to ask if I was OK. I assured her I was and apologized for not letting her know what had happened.

After I hung up the phone, I couldn't sleep, so I picked up the book I was reading, Willa Cather's *My Antonia*, and read until I came to the part about the ranch hand losing his ears to frostbite in a Nebraska blizzard.

Inside the snow caves on Mount Rainier, we huddled next to each other. There were three of us in the cave I was in and two in both of the other caves. The caves muffled the storm, protecting us from its violence. We were out of the wind and were warmer, although lying in the snow, we could feel the coldness on our backs and hips. It was dark, although we had enough light to see each other, and we exchanged concerned glances. Mostly we were silent. With our fate hanging on the whims of the storm, there was little we could say that would be meaningful.

We took turns checking on the storm, hoping to see a break below that would allow us to return to the hut.

One hour passed.

Another.

We had solved the problem of the storm, and we were all safe, but it was unsettling not knowing what might happen, how long we might be trapped, or if we would have to spend the night in the cave. I remembered the moments of fear when my car ran off the road in Nebraska. I could have died in that cold. Now that feeling was back as I hunched inside the cave.

It was not death. We all die. It was not the method of death. That seems rather unimportant when we look at it realistically. It was not a fear of death itself or a fear of any hereafter. It was a fear of not living anymore, not being able to fulfill the dreams which qualify a life as complete.

I looked out the opening of the cave at the still-threatening storm. Life can't stop now. There's too much left undone. Too many mountains, both figurative and literal, left to climb. Too many stories to write and books to read, places to go and friends to enjoy. I had to have more.

It had been two in the afternoon when we started digging the caves. At five, the storm showed no sign of giving up. At seven, the cave became lighter inside. Bill, our leader, wriggled out the narrow opening.

"It's all over," he shouted. We hurried out to see the peak of Little Tahoma three thousand feet below us. We could start down.

For five hours we had been trapped. It took two more hours to wind our way across the Ingraham Glacier, textured with gaping crevasses, down the scree slope below Cathedral Rocks, and across the Emmons Glacier to the safety of the stone hut at Camp Muir.

There, just before dark, we collapsed into grateful unconsciousness.

© 2022 by Andie Thrams

De Scandere Virtute*

Chris Kalman

I must stoop to take
an uncommon opinion
regarding the purported

virtue of this climbing *thing*—
passion, lifestyle, sport, what
have you—many of us hold

in common esteem; must pause
to question *de scandere virtute,*
if you will. The thing is

(granite aside, which hides
the truth in a magma amalgam
of mineral soup)

if there's one thing we can learn
from rock, it's this: it's nothing
more than eon upon eon of flesh

and bone turned to strata after
strata of stone—each band
a story lived long ago

for the blink of an eye,
just to be forgotten, nothing
more than the deeds of dead

dinosaurs—coelacanths, gastro-
pods and the like—just
like empires, here

then *poof*—gone—in the blink
of an eye. I'm telling you,
Jeffers was right

when he called stone-
cutters "fore-defeated
challengers of oblivion"

or Shelley, who knew
(of sand and stone) a
thing or two.

The guts, the gore, the glory:
so much stardust in the
swirling whorl of time.

The climb, the top, the story:
a sigh in the wind. Just
give it time.

* Latin for "the virtue of climbing."

Buried

Edmond Stevens

The Sevier Desert disperses west to the Nevada State Line and is assumed by authorities to be where Josh Powell buried his wife's body before moving off to Washington where he eventually torched his house, killing himself and two sons. If a task force of police, cadaver dogs, National Guard, and volunteers had never been able to find Susan Powell in all this wilderness, then Trey knew he was on the right course.

The idea of an unrecovered body left Trey morbidly unsettled. Muggs Stump, and later Seth Shaw, friends from his apprentice years of climbing, had both been crushed under a shear of ice on the Denali glacier. Trey had stood at the edge of crevasses in Alaska, the Andes, and the Himalayas, mystical and unfathomable gyri, deeper in places than ocean trenches. Every few months he had the same dream of being buried, illuminated by the dim indigo light penetrating the glacial strata, waiting season after season for friends to come back and release him from the icy resin.

Trey left I-15 at Nephi and turned west. First Leamington, then Fool Creek Reservoir, Sugarvillle, and the turnoff into the Sevier watershed. No question, he'd timed it badly, leaving the house as the last dabs of sunlight had torched the highest peaks of the Wasatch. To add to the foolishness, he hadn't packed food. People in these parts rose early to work the fields or the mineral processing plants, so the diners and coffee shops were dark by seven. He could have brought a cooler, but the back of the 4Runner, now topping two-hundred-and-fifty-thousand miles, was packed halfway to the headliner, the passenger seat stacked with ropes and a bivy sack.

This past week word had come from Everest Base Camp that a local climber had died on his way down from the summit. The story in the *Trib* said that the Sherpas weren't able to bring down the remains. Families often question why a body cannot be lowered from the summit flanks, but at extreme altitude, even the simplest tasks increase by magnitudes. Lowering a body would involve a cat's cradle of ropes, pulleys, and a team of four or five Sherpas, already spent from their summit support. Standard practice for death at high altitude is to zip the body into a sleeping bag and push it off the main bootpack. It joins the frozen ossuary a thousand feet below, honoring the tradition of burial at sea but with the body committed to the mountain.

He hadn't known the dead climber, though they'd probably pushed carts past each other at Harmon's or Home Depot, sat in folding chairs at an avalanche seminar, or stood in line for the first lift on opening day at Alta. Such anonymous proximity was not unusual. The climbing world breaks down into two small cultures. There were the dirt bags, living out of vans or garage conversions, working in gear shops or, if lucky, teaching and guiding. Then there were the client climbers, maybe a hedge fund guy, cardio doc, or software startup guru. Not exclusively a culture of men, either. Trey had guided power women on demanding high-altitude slogs while the men were left behind, sheltering in their sleeping bags back at base camp. Though his client set was often people of means, Trey didn't deny these patron climbers their chops. Your wealth portfolio doesn't give a leg up on a vertical rock face or jugging up a hanging glacier, functioning on fifty percent of the oxygen folks require for stair climbing or grocery hauling at sea level. Climbers of all stripes earn their summit moment.

When he hit Sugarville around nine, every storefront was dark, not even the usual neon soda and oil filter signage. If Josh Powell had driven through after dark, his boys asleep and Susan's body wrapped in a tarp or carpet, he would have passed without a single witness to assist the police investigation.

A number of dirt roads fork off State 174. One continues north to Topaz Mountain where gem hunters pay a fee for a pick and bucket to prospect for semi-precious minerals. Families come to overturn rocks and shift the soil, hoping to extract crystal gemstones. Trey had gone into the night on a mission not so differently from Josh Powell, planning a burial isolated from traveled landscape and prospecting tourists. He chose the road west into the Salina badlands.

Few mysteries are more troubling than a missing body with their unfinished stories and questions about the final minutes. His friends, Scott and Kyle, went missing several years before on Ogre l in Pakistan's Karakoram. Did they fall or die of exposure? Did one have the chance to save himself at the cost of leaving the other behind, surviving with the lifetime guilt of abandoning a partner? What was that poem he'd had to memorize in junior high and the part he could not shake as he aspired to climb high, exposed places? "The many men, so beautiful! And they all dead did lie: And a thousand thousand slimy things lived on; and so did I."

Family is a big deal in the Utah Mormon culture. Even when it comes to murder. Josh's father, Steven, had an unnatural infatuation with his daughter-in-law, including furtive videos and photos. Brother Michael was believed to have been an accomplice, if not in the murder, possibly in the disposal of the body. All three Powell men were now dead, Steven of natural causes after serving seven years for possessing child pornography, and Michael, stepping off the roof of a parking structure after investigators seemed to be closing the circle. The Powells took the secret of Susan's whereabouts to their graves, providing no peace to her parents who would never have the closure of a proper burial of their daughter's remains. As a member of the Salt Lake Search and Rescue team, Trey would have surely volunteered to be part of the search team, but he was guiding Aconcagua that December.

For months now, Trey had thought about giving away his climbing gear. It was a weighty question, as grave and consequential as donating an organ. As a donor, some part of you goes on living in the skin of another. The idea that somebody could take a fall off a poorly placed ice screw, or a partner be dropped by an unlocked carabiner, was more responsibility than he wanted to take on. If somebody was going to fuck up and die, at least it wouldn't be on his gear.

Trey steered into a break in the fence line. The tires of the Toyota thrummed as he rolled over the bars of a cattle guard, a horizontal grid of steel pipes over a trench. Even with a fifteen-foot-wide gap in the fence and verdant grazing on the other side, cows balked at crossing. In the bovine processing center, the cow dismisses the bars and sees only the bottom of the trench. Trey's ex, or more correctly his ex-ex, given that they'd been married twice, argued that he and his cohort had the mental capacity of cattle. But she had it wrong. Climbers learn to acknowledge the trench but trust the bars. Lately, though, Trey saw only the trench.

His headlights punched holes in the darkness, moving tubes of light over the rutted Jeep track, the creosote and brittlebush swatting the side panels of the 4Runner. Veering sharply left or right might plunge him over hidden bluffs or mire him in the chalky washes. *Just keep in the matched grooves of the Jeep track, Trey, and you'll be fine.*

Creeping up a similar Jeep track, Josh Powell's Chrysler van would have been tossed and bounced, though it was hard to believe that Powell's two sleeping sons, four and six, wouldn't have been jarred awake by the jolting van, wondering where their dad was taking them in the middle of the night. But then a kid doesn't have much experience to go by; the world is what their parents tell them it is. If Dad said they were going camping, a regular family activity, of course they'd believe him, even at two in the morning without the usual kit of tent, stove, and sleeping bags.

Trey reached the crest of a moderate grade, braked, and stepped out. Moving around the 4Runner, extending the circle in wider arcs, he assessed that he'd arrived at some kind of prominence, only a hundred feet above the landscape but secure from the sweeping erosion of any flash flood. This would do.

He back-and-forthed the truck, parking crosswise over the Jeep track, and switched to the parking lights, sufficient to dig by but not stand out like an airport beacon in the dark. This was definite midnight business, giving the task a feeling of something criminal. Trey lowered the rear liftgate and pulled the shovel from the heaps of gear. As best he could see in the dimmed parking lights, the near landscape was strewn with broken fragments of limestone from ancient upheavals when the Great Basin had been submerged beneath an inland sea.

Calculating the volume of his stash, he was going to have to clear an area the size of a hot tub. He wondered if Josh Powell thought to bring a shovel into the desert. Surely the kids would have remembered a detail like that. The tip of Trey's shovel barely chipped the baked surface crust. Every time the blade struck a rock, it rang with a ricochet shot that would have surely awakened a sleeping child. Josh Powell was sloppy and impulsive, not one for thinking in the big picture. When Susan hadn't responded to calls from worried family, they visited the Powell home and found two box fans left churning in the living room and a large wet stain on the sofa. Detectives later uncovered Susan's phone in the crease of the seats in the Chrysler van and found it incredible that Josh would take his boys camping in a threatening blizzard when he was scheduled to work just hours later. He'd explain to police that he'd thought it was Sunday rather than Monday, though in the LDS culture, Sunday is the tentpole from which the week is hung.

Beneath the surface crust, the earth gave up more easily and Trey moved scoops of sand and decomposing limestone to either side. He was tossing, by his count, twenty thousand dollars in gear. Not that it had all come out-of-pocket. In exchange for using his image in their ads, or for appearances at trade shows, companies had provided a lot for free or at cost. Still, he could have recouped a good piece of change by recycling it at any of the sports consignment shops around Salt Lake.

Sweat sheeted down the inside of his fleece hoodie, in spite of the desert air close to freezing. Removing the layer, he continued to dig in a sleeveless tee. With every jab of the shovel, an electric shock fired up his arm into his surgically-restored shoulder, the result of a sixty-foot fall at Smith Rocks. Each twist on his twice-reconstructed knee sent a boring ache into the joint. Every half dozen scoops, he had to pause and shake one hand from the wrist to restore sensation, damaged from frostbite after a blizzard on the retreat from Mt. Robson. In spite of chronic injuries, Trey was expedition-fit, yet this was still a labor. For sure Josh, a cubical creature in financial services, would not have had the endurance to move this much dirt. Josh would have likely searched for a depression in the earth and covered the body with slabs, sufficiently heavy not to be disturbed by desert predators.

A body is no easy thing to disappear. Even glaciers and avalanches give up their victims. Trey and his sister had dispersed their father's ashes on the ninth fairway at Torrey Pines. Riding in the golf cart, tipping the Ziplock bags just inside the rough, Trey realized he was leaving a chalk stripe like the third base line at Dodger Stadium. They had to quickly backtrack and scrub the ashes into the grass, nervous that they might be prosecuted for disposal of human remains on private property.

Salt Lake detectives had gained access to Susan's emails to friends, expressing fears of her violent husband. Investigators found a video cautioning that in the event of her death by any cause, they should consider it a homicide. Susan's parents later told police that then-five-year-old Braden drew a picture of a van with three people inside. He told his teacher that "Mommy was in the trunk," though there was no real trunk in the van, and psychologists worried that Braden's memory had been overwritten by all the press and hearsay.

With no evidence of a body, and conflicting testimony, deputies and detectives finally closed the investigation. Because of an ongoing legal dispute with Susan's parents over her life insurance, the courts had yet to declare Susan legally dead. She remained in a category with Muggs and Seth and Scott and Kyle. Unknown. Without the evidence of a body, the best the authorities could do was to make a presumption of death by other than natural causes. Maybe this Josh and Susan Powell thing was an absurd fixation, but then he'd become obsessed with the idea of unfinished lives.

Trey finally hit a limestone slab, and without a breaker bar or pick, he wasn 't going any deeper. This would have to do.

With the equipment transferred to the pit, he returned to the Toyota for a half dozen jugs of industrial drain cleaner and doused the pile. The sodium hydroxide would eat into the aluminum of the cams and stoppers, rendering them useless. The caustic chemicals would also saturate the ropes and slings, and they'd quickly fray and shred. Nobody was going to climb on this gear ever again. He backfilled the hole and returned a few rocks to the top of the excavation to blend with the landscape. Trey stepped back from his work, starting to pick out vague contours in the failing darkness.

Where are you, Muggs and Seth, Scott and Kyle? Where are you, Susan? Another season, another year would pass without an answer.

He pitched the shovel into the Toyota, and then the empty drain cleaner jugs, in keeping with the wilderness-user's ethic of "leave no trace." He closed up, climbed behind the wheel, and rotated the 4Runner, careful not to back into a wash. He didn't need to call a tow truck and create a lot of questions about what the hell he was doing out here. Cautiously, following the twin ruts, he reached the cattle guard, then switched on the high beams.

Trey turned back toward Nephi and the Interstate, knowing that one of the cafes would be open to feed the early shift. His first impulse was to fill the void with food. Beyond that, he'd have to contemplate what life would look like now without the badge that defined him. One thing a climber learns from experience is that gravity always wins. He'd decided to come off the mountain and learn to live in the valley. He would now have to look deep into that void and acknowledge he no longer saw the sense in what he'd been doing. If a life could have a crux, then this was surely his.

In the middle of that thought, the swirling red and blue lights of a police car appeared on his rear bumper. Trey coasted over to the gravel shoulder. He checked off the steps of the drill with the conscious order of placing a climbing anchor: Hands in sight on the steering wheel; where was his wallet and license, what was his story for what he was doing out here? He could say he'd been out camping, but like Josh, with no sleeping bag or tent in the vehicle, his statement would sound immediately flimsy.

A Millard County sheriff approached from the rear, seeming to take note of the dust and mud coating the wheels and side panels.

Trey lowered the side window. "Morning, officer."

In the rearview mirror, Trey identified another police vehicle pulled up behind the first cruiser.

"Is it okay if I take my hands off the wheel and get out my license and registration?"

"Just keep 'em up where I can see 'em," the deputy said, more a function of procedure than intimidation.

The second officer moved up along the slanted gravel of the shoulder on the passenger side, raising a flashlight to illuminate the cargo area of the 4Runner. The deputy stepped back to confer with the second officer at the tailgate, who again raised the beam to light the cargo area. The first cop returned to the driver's side window.

"I see a shovel back there and a lot of dirt. And what's them jugs? You want to explain what kinda activities you've been up to out here in the night?"

The second deputy moved out to the center of the road just off the rear quarter panel, a defensive maneuver to cover his partner.

"Just driving." Trey was careful to scrub any traces of guilt or complicity from his voice.

The deputy swung open the door and Trey recognized the boxy snout of the police sidearm. "Outside," he ordered, then stepped back and gestured to the asphalt. "On the ground."

Trey raised his hands and rotated off the driver's seat and moved to where the cop pointed with his sidearm, dropping to his knees.

"All the way. Face down and spread 'em." The deputy tipped him face forward.

Trey reached out to soften contact with the asphalt, but still gravel fragments drilled into his palms and cheek. Every climber accepts the proposition of abrupt contact with the earth, but eventually the ground always comes up in ways never expected.

"What kind of digging you been doing out here anyway? Something you were thinking to bury where nobody'd find it?"

Trey knew the answer was obvious. *Yeah,* he thought. *Bodies.*

He didn't struggle or resist the cuffs. It seemed fitting. Others were dead and lost, and he had to answer why he was still alive, still here among the other slimy things.

No Comment

Marc Beaudin

> *Never let a few facts*
> *get in the way of a good story*
> —Ed Abbey (as quoted by Doug Peacock)

Somewhere south of Salt Lake
& north of Jalisco
east of the Hollywood sign
& west of this Gila Woodpecker
digging a new home in the arm of a cactus,
Doug & I sit at Abbey's grave
passing a warm can of *cerveza*
between the three of us

The bird doesn't mind the intrusion
Visitations here are rare &
sometimes among the gifts
of shells & stones & hand-carved effigies
something is left that's
of use in lining a nest

I've brought a heart-shaped stone
to which I've tied a small black feather
The woodpecker eyes the string
as we finish our beer
& say our goodbyes

At this point the ornithologists
are rising in protest
because Gila Woodpeckers don't line their nest
with string or anything else
so the entire conceit of this poem
falls apart, to which I say,
quoting the words carved
into the rock marking his grave,

"No Comment"

Graduate Student Essay Contest Winners

Each year, in keeping with our mission to promote emerging writers, *Deep Wild Journal* sponsors a no-fee contest for student writers. This year's focus, an essay contest for graduate students, garnered entries from coast to coast. We are pleased to announce the winners:

First Place
"An Ordinary Day"
Kelsey Wellington, Lindenwood University

Second Place
"Betweenness"
Chelsey Waters, Eastern Oregon University

Third Place
"How to Botch a Funding Award"
Kalle Fox, University of Montana

Honorable Mentions:
- "The Cradle." Meghan Harrison, Western Carolina University
- "Go West, Young Man: Reimagining Gender on the Pacific Crest Trail." Maddie Melton, University of Utah.
- "Swimming among Mountain Tops." Hannah L. Coble, University of Minnesota
- "Land of Many Uses." Mikaela Osler, University of New Mexico

According to Corrinne Brumby, one of the contest judges, "These essays were thoughtful and challenged us to relate to the wild in new and deeper ways, considering not only the impact we have on wilderness, but especially the impact it has on us. Ultimately the wild natural world in all its fierce, raw, beauty changes us."

Our thanks go out to the many graduate students who sent us their work. We wish we could have honored more of them! Cash awards for the top three essays are $250, $100, and $50, and all winners and Honorable Mentions will receive copies of the journal. Look for Kalle Fox's Third Place essay on the *Deep Wild* website this summer. Essays were judged anonymously by Alaskan writer Marybeth Holleman and *Deep Wild* Assistant Editor Corrinne Brumby.

Deep Wild 2022 Graduate Student Essay Contest
First Place

An Ordinary Day

Kelsey Wellington

I stared up at the cloudless cerulean sky, oblivious to the numbing snow that enveloped my body, and let out an agonized groan.

"No, no, *no,*" I whispered aloud to myself, each *no* sounding more desperate than the last.

The *pop.* I'd heard it as I fell. My skis went one way, my body the other, and my right knee had popped. There was no mistaking that sound; it was every skier's worst nightmare.

I shut my eyes to the dazzling day and began counting my breaths.

Inhale through the nose, two, three.

Exhale through the mouth, two, three.

"Are you okay?" came Brian's voice from downslope.

My mind was racing. *This is not happening. This is* not *happening, not again.*

Twenty seconds ago, I had a calendar full of outdoor adventures spanning the entire year. Some of my plans required months of training. A few were going to be crowned my biggest achievements in the outdoors, assuming I pulled them off. Skiing the Skillet Glacier on Mount Moran, one of the fifty classic ski descents in North America. Thirty-, forty-, even seventy-mile runs through the Absaroka-Beartooth Wilderness and the Wind River Range. Climbing trips to Wyoming, California, Nevada, Greece. Mountain biking with my father in Utah.

Now, I had nothing. It all vanished with one bad ski turn. The *pop*—the sound made when an ACL, the band of tissue in the knee that connects femur to tibia, tears. An injury that requires half a year to marginally recover from, and a full year to return to normal activity. A year that friends have described as being one of the darker times in their lives.

I wanted to scream. Because of the *pop*, because of how perfect the day had been until this moment, because of how close we were to the base of our chosen ski descent, because I barely knew my ski partner, because I couldn't handle another injury. *Not again,* I thought. *Not. Again.*

I heard Brian shuffling through the snow down the hill from where I lay, likely trying to get to me.

My eyes flew open. "I'm okay!" I shouted to assuage his worries, my voice lacking conviction. I was not okay. This situation was bad, and the longer I lay here, the more tenuous things were going to get.

This is no time for wallowing, I reminded myself. *You are still in the mountains. You are still five miles from the trailhead.* I rolled onto my right side and attempted to unwind my crossed skis, which faced up the hill from where my head lay, but that motion sent a searing fire up my right leg.

I bit back a scream, not wanting to frighten Brian.

Instead of moving my legs, I would have to move my torso. I attempted a sit-up, but the weight of my pack held me down.

Brian called my name again.

"One sec!" I shouted back, then threw my arms up and lunged up towards my feet. I managed to grab one of my ski boots, leverage I then used to pull myself into an awkward sitting position. I felt the cold from the snow slowly seeping through my ski bibs, so I worked quickly to unclip my boots from my ski bindings. Then I curled my knees toward my chest—more fire in the right leg—and spun around to face down the slope. Leaning on my ski poles, I managed to stand up in the deep snow, but my right leg immediately buckled. I gritted my teeth, holding back another scream.

God. Fucking. Dammit.

"Hey," Brian said when he saw me poke above the snow. "You okay?"

I stared at him, measuring the weight of what I needed to say. We barely knew each other, having met only two days prior in a yoga class at our local climbing gym. As we'd hiked our way six and a half miles up Big St. Joe Peak on our backcountry skis this morning, we had discussed a range of topics, but no amount of information about how many siblings the other had or what each other's favorite food was would gauge how each of us would respond in a backcountry emergency.

I took a breath. "I think I just blew out my knee."

I watched as Brian's face worked through a range of emotions in the span of three seconds. Shock. Disbelief. Fear. Worry. That *holyshitareyouserious* feeling. And finally, resolve.

He set his stubbled jaw, unclipped from his ski bindings, and began crawling up the hill in thigh-deep snow to where I stood. "Let's just take a minute to breathe, okay?"

I shook my head. "I need to get down," I responded sternly "Now."

Brian began to speak.

"The longer I sit here," I cut him off, "the more the adrenaline is going to wear off, and then it's going to hurt like hell." I pointed to the flat section that marked the start of our initial uphill climb three hours earlier. It couldn't be more than a hundred feet away. "I'm going to butt-scoot my way down to flat ground, then we can reassess." I didn't want to think about the fact that we were still five miles from the parking lot, in the remote Selway-Bitterroot Wilderness south of Missoula, MT, with no cell service, no emergency beacon, and not another soul around.

I looked my ski partner in the eyes—gorgeous aquamarine pools that had swayed me into asking for his number—and nodded. A light breeze tousled his shoulder-length auburn hair, and I resisted the urge to tuck strands of it behind his ear. This was absolutely *not* the time to flirt.

He swallowed and nodded back, then busied himself with collecting my pack and skis as I slid on my butt down the last one hundred feet of our approximately 5,000-foot descent.

When I reached the floor of the Bass Creek drainage, I heard voices coming from the west. Then, two men appeared from around a bend in the trail, on their way back to their cars after a day of backcountry skiing. They stopped when they saw me, standing, leaning on ski poles, wearing ski boots, with no skis in sight.

"Are you okay?" one of them asked.

I smiled. "Oh, I think I tore my ACL back there," I replied, pointing up the slope.

"Oh shit," the men said in unison, and immediately dropped their packs, unclipped from their skis, and rushed over to me. As they came closer, one of the men looked familiar—Donny, my good friend's fiancé, had the same kind eyes, the same blonde scruff, the same deep voice. But no, this was a remote corner of Montana's backcountry, on the outskirts of a town I'd left three years ago. I hadn't seen Donny in all that time. I pushed the thought away.

"My ski partner is up there," I said, gesturing to the gully I just slid down from. "He's getting my gear." I slowly lowered myself to the ground, gingerly maneuvering around my now very stiff knee, and sat upright in the snow, my left leg bent, my right leg straight.

The pair began assessing my injury, asking me questions about how it happened, did I hear a pop, what was my range of motion like? As I responded, Brian made his way down the slope, shouldering two packs and two pairs of skis, his body sinking in the snow up to his thighs with every step.

"Donny," one of the men said, "what do you think about splinting her leg?"

"*Donny!*" I half-shrieked.

The man with the kind eyes, blonde scruff, and deep voice looked up, startled. As he stared at me, I watched recognition creep into his expression, and he smiled. "Well, well," he said, "if it isn't the most accident-prone gal I know."

I offered him a half-smile, then glanced down at my watch. It was two in the afternoon. Brian and I should have been nearly back to our cars by now. On skis, the five-mile trek out would have taken us half an hour at the most. Instead, the last fifteen minutes had been eaten up by my injury, and it would be many hours before we'd see the parking lot, likely under the heavy blanket of dark.

I listened as the men debated my options for safely getting back to the trailhead.

"We could tie p-cord around the tips of her skis, and you could ski behind her, Brian. Kind of like a leash," Chuck, Donny's ski partner, said. "That way you can control her speed and guide her turns."

Brian shook his head. "I don't have long enough p-cord for that."

"Can we somehow fashion a sled out of skis and our avalanche shovels?" Donny wondered.

"Guys," I chimed in, "I think I can ski out."

All three men laughed.

"No way."

"Absolutely not."

"Very funny."

The adrenaline coursing through my body seemed to replace the logic and common sense I once possessed, and I began to protest, so convinced of my own abilities that I fully believed this plan could work. Hadn't I already proven that I could do hard things? Hadn't my years spent playing in and getting hurt in the backcountry been enough evidence? I could ski out. I *needed* to ski out. The thought of the steadily encroaching night, the steadily dropping temperatures, and my steadily worsening pain turned my blood to ice. Despite its very high potential for disaster, a thirty-minute ski out seemed like a far better option.

"The second you put any lateral force on your knee," Brian said, "like stopping or turning on skis, you're going to be in a lot of pain. And you'll probably make it worse."

I lay back in the snow and shut my eyes. "When I said I love suffering," I said, "this is *not* what I meant."

"What do you mean, you love suffering?" Brian asked hours earlier as we zig-zagged our way up the mountain.

"The longer the mileage, the greater the elevation gain, and the more exhausted my body, the happier I am," I replied. "There is no greater feeling than knowing my own body carried me all that way. And there is no better teacher than the backcountry. The mountains are amazing teachers of suffering."

I was ahead of my ski partner, breaking trail through the heavy, sunbaked snow, but I imagined him shaking his head behind me. "So, what you're saying is, you're a masochist."

"Isn't any mountain athlete? I mean, even a little bit?"

"Something tells me you're a special breed, though," Brian said.

I sighed and opened my eyes, basking in the deep blue of the sky. A perfect, ordinary day. At least, it had been. I took a breath, hating myself for what I was about to say, for getting myself into this mess in the first place.

"I have to walk out," I said.

These were the words everyone had already been thinking—I knew that—but they needed to come from me. Friend or not, asking someone with an obliterated knee to walk five miles out of the woods, through deep snow, all while wearing ski boots, is no small thing.

A collective sigh came from the men. They all nodded. The seriousness of my situation weighed heavily on our collective shoulders.

"Fine," I grunted, sitting up and thrusting out my mittened hand. "Give me some Tylenol to get the ball rolling."

Chuck fished around in his pack while Brian searched for a branch to use as a splint.

"Just in case," Donny said, handing me his Garmin inReach Mini, an emergency locator beacon that would trigger a rescue operation with one push of a button.

I was determined not to push the *SOS* button, but I thanked Donny all the same. Brian and I would get out of here without a rescue, even if we endured both a sunset and a sunrise before we reached the trailhead.

Brian returned with a foot-and-a-half long alder branch and set to work splinting it against my knee with ski straps and ACE bandages. I downed Tylenol and continued cracking jokes at my own expense, hoping to keep the creeping sense of devastation at bay.

I couldn't go through this again—being injured. I couldn't endure another season—a season reserved for long trail runs, alpine climbs, and week-long backpacking trips, all the things that brought me alive—on the sidelines. The last six years of my life seemed defined by my injuries. Broken hand, broken ankle, torn pulley tendons in my fingers, broken foot, umbilical hernia, torn rotator cuff, permanent cold-induced nerve damage in both feet, dislocated fingers, torn biceps tendon. And now, blown-out knee. I was utterly exhausted by it all. The doctor's visits, the physical therapy appointments, the months lost to recovery, the plans put on hold, the piling medical bills. Didn't the mountains know that all I wanted was to be surrounded by their intimidating peaks, to dip my toes in their alpine lakes, to watch the sunrise set their spires on fire? Why did I keep having to prove myself in their presence?

I felt my face growing hot with emotion, and I swallowed back a sob. "The folks at Missoula Bone and Joint are going to lose their minds when I walk through their doors again," I said, trying to banish my disappointment.

"It's funny that you think you'll walk in," Donny retorted.

Laughter rang through the drainage.

The splint wasn't perfect, but it did the job. My knee hardly bent, and my stiffened leg was able to bear my weight with only minor pain, but maybe the latter was just the Tylenol kicking in. I took a few steps, leaning hard into my ski poles. Nothing buckled or gave way; I didn't feel any fire burn through my leg, only a dull ache.

I took a deep breath. "Okay," I said, determination creeping into my voice. "Let's get out of here."

Brian used his remaining ski straps to tether both pairs of skis to each other, then strapped them to his ski pack, which he slung over his shoulders. Then he hung my pack over his shoulders in reverse so that it hung down over his chest. Discomfort oozed from his stance.

I looked at Donny and Chuck, their packs now full of our unnecessary equipment—avalanche shovels, probes, and beacons—and felt my eyes welling with tears. The last thirty minutes had been some of the most intense of my life, and I had shared it with near-strangers. Their generosity would have brought me to my knees if I hadn't already done that on my own.

"I—," I began to say, but the words caught in my throat. I was speechless for the first time all day.

"You would have done the same for us," Donny said, reading my mind. "With one exception: there's no way in hell I'd be in such good spirits if our roles were reversed. You're a champ."

The men laughed. I shrugged. It never occurred to me that falling apart was an option. That would come later, after a two-hour hike out filled with personal stories, flirtatious jokes, and the occasional wince of pain; after parking lot beers left by Donny and Chuck on the hood of my car; after celebrating the fact that we made it out before sunset; after phone calls to my dog-sitter and my roommate; after the forty-five minute drive home in which I laughed with Brian and pleaded with the world to keep reality at bay for just a little while longer; after waving goodbye to my ski partner on my front porch; after finally shutting my door to the outside world. Only then would I fall apart, a mess of tears and snot and streaked mascara, a cacophony of wailing and hiccupping and screaming, on the living room carpet.

But here in the backcountry, none of that would do any good. *The mountains don't care*—the first lesson every outdoor recreationist learns. The mountains didn't care about my body, my goals, my hopes and dreams, my plans, my loved ones, my emotions. Devastation meant nothing to the eras-old granite spires that stood tall around us.

In the decade I had spent exploring mountains—running across whole ranges, climbing their tallest peaks, skiing their narrow couloirs, biking their winding trails—they had become my greatest teachers. I learned about all-consuming grief when friends were lost to the mountains, and I learned about resilience when I returned to the same mountains in search of peace. When the weather turned, when the temperature dropped, when the unexpected happened, I learned to adapt, to change course, even to walk away. With every mile further, with every foot higher, I learned how to endure, how to suffer, how to push myself. Over time, I became an immovable, unyielding, inexorable force.

Just like the mountains.

So, I shrugged, met Donny's eyes, and said, "I don't know any other way to be."

He smiled.

With my leg feeling stable, my pain under control, and all our gear on Brian's shoulders, he and I were ready to make the long trek out. We turned to Donny and Chuck and began the process of seeing them off, thanking them, insisting we would be fine without them, promising to text when we made it safely out, making loose plans to grab beers when this was all over.

As the pair skied down the trail, I sighed. "This is going to suck," I said flatly.

Brian nodded.

"Some first date, huh?" I joked.

He smiled.

A joke came to mind, and I burst into laughter at my own wit.

"What's so funny?" Brian asked.

When I collected myself, I said, "I guess you could say something about you brings me to my knees."

But no. Only the mountains ever had that power.

© 2022 by Andie Thrams

Deep Wild 2022 Graduate Student Essay Contest
Second Place

Betweenness

Chelsey Waters

1. Floating

I tucked the oar handles under my knees and leaned back, stretching my spine. It felt compacted from the boat dropping into the troughs and watery holes in Fiddle. Fiddle came on the heels of Traps and Chair, all three rapids in quick succession, and some ways ahead lay the last rapids, Black Rock. Here, though, the tailwaves flattened and the river entered a long, calm stretch. We all needed a stretch. "You can swim here," I told my clients, and they slipped or flipped or dived into the river, eager to exit the heat. They looked like so many fishing bobbers, just their heads and the shoulders of their life jackets above the surface. Charlie's clients did the same, and for a while he and I spun slowly in the current, alone in our boats but grinning at each other, at our stupid luck: to spend our summers here, existing in this space between wet and dry, between water and sky, between the fish and the birds and the two walls of this colossal canyon.

Charlie and I go way back. His grandpa guided the first trip I went on when I was six. The Middle Fork of the Salmon River—a hundred miles of whitewater and fat trout and my mother's white knuckles gripping my lifejacket, her eyes closed in prayer while the waves baptized me in my state of open-mouthed delight. It was there that I caught my first fish and met Charlie and fell a bit in love, mostly with the river.

When he was eighteen, Charlie got a job rafting, and a couple years later, he contacted me after a fellow guide called it quits to get married. Why would he leave—why would *anyone,* we wondered, floating through those summers, no longer children and not yet saddled with adult concerns, even as our time in college edged toward an end.

We were existing in a state of betweenness, and we felt the temporal nature of it even as we were somewhat unaware of its existence. Anthropologists describe betweenness as a liminal state that exists during a transition or rite of passage. It can be deeply formative and rewarding, but betweenness comes with drawbacks—one of which is a distinct lack of power and agency.

As guides, we were visible—driving the bus, giving safety talks, answering questions—and invisible, rowing from the stern of the rafts and unnecessary or uninvited to most of our clients' conversations. We had the authority to utter commands about when to paddle and when to get back in the boat, but we also served at our clients' pleasure. We didn't have much money or say over our schedules, but we didn't especially mind. There's solace in a shared sense of not yet belonging.

Perhaps I should note that Charlie and I did not date. Temperamentally, we were unsuited, combustible off the water. Instead, we fell into an undefined state of intimacy, in the manner of people who've grown up reading each other's thoughts. Spinning on the boats that day as our clients bobbed along, we recognized the same delight in each other's faces, as well as desire, that we could exist in this place—this river and this betweenness—forever.

Which a river would never allow. It carries you, buries you, holds you for a minute in a good hole and maybe pins you to a rock you meant to miss, but it doesn't keep you for long. So at the end of our day trips, after we passed the bend where the last rapids tried to grind us against the cliff face and as the boat ramp at Lucile came into view, it was always accompanied by a sense that things were ending a little too soon. Charlie's parents had divorced and mine had moved from my childhood hometown—out of the state, in fact—and the river, mercurial as it was, seemed like the one constant in our lives.

Maybe I felt I belonged to the river because I'd grown up in the interstices, in a place that was not quite urban but not fully rural, in the middle of a state, Idaho, that demanded allegiance to its north or south. Charlie was likewise caught between his love for this wild place and an urban upbringing, pursuing a career that would require him to give up the river.

Not that day, though. That day we backed the trailer down the ramp and loaded the boats. Soon we were on the highway, windows down, the wind pulling the heat and moisture from our bodies except for where we remained sweat-stuck to the vinyl seats as Riggins came into view.

2. Riggins

If you draw a line across the center of Idaho, Riggins is nearly smack dab in the middle. It's about 300 miles north to Canada or south to Nevada, and a bridge at the edge of town marks the point where Idaho splits in the temporal sense, too, the northern half being on Pacific time and the southern half on Mountain. Of course, the river has its own time zone—sunup to sundown. River time. I never wore a watch.

A sign on the way into town welcomes you to "the whitewater capital of Idaho," and in the summers I worked there, that sign was still pretty shiny. Like so many towns in this state—in the West, in the world—Riggins has had to assume new identities with time. Adapt or die.

Though I suppose being a ghost is also a sort of betweenness, another liminal state.

Many Nez Perce, the Nimiipuu, wintered in this valley, enjoying its relatively temperate climate and, I like to think, the hot springs a mile or two upstream from where the town now sits. They were driven out, slowly by miners and then officially in 1877 when the U.S. Army, violating the terms of an 1855 treaty, burned the tribe's winter food caches and chased the Nimiipuu nearly to Canada. A small band escaped over the border, but those who didn't, and who hadn't already been killed or starved, were captured and imprisoned in Kansas and later sent to Oklahoma. Some made it back to Idaho in later years, to live on a reservation a fraction of the size of their homeland.

White settlers landed in Riggins during the mining boom, sluicing for gold. Some mine openings are still visible along the highway, as well as triangular piles of tailings that look like half-buried Egyptian pyramids, prone to landslides and partly grown over with clumps of sage and seedy elderberries.

On day trips, a few miles in, we'd pull to the west side of the river and guide clients through sage and invasive cheat grass to the remains of a small rock house—one room, maybe ten feet by fifteen feet, the timbered roof long ago collapsed—that, legend has it, belonged to a white mine owner, his name perhaps lost to history. River stories, like most oral traditions, are part truth and part myth. We've been told that the low pit near the house is where the white owner's workers—Chinese miners, possibly enslaved, or if not, probably indentured—would have slept huddled together for warmth in the winter. Then the U.S. drove out the Chinese, too, with the 1882 Chinese Exclusion Act, a legislative work of overt racism that wouldn't be overturned for 61 years.

As the mining dried up, ranching and agriculture expanded, and then the run on timber started. In the aftermath of World War II, Riggins reinvented itself as a logging town, a sawmill mushrooming on the narrow point where the Salmon River and the Little Salmon River conjoin. The mill processed white pine and fir until it burned in 1982.

Riggins's population dipped over 15 percent in the following years, from 557 to 443, a loss it has not regained—unless you count summers. In the summers people like Charlie and me nearly doubled the population. Except in rare cases, rafting is a seasonal job. Many of us were college students between academic years, but a sizeable population included ski bums between seasons, teachers between paychecks, or slightly older folks between careers—neophytes, no matter our age. We joined, temporarily, an aging town populace of retirees and folks who found themselves in a similarly liminal space: no longer a mill town, not quite a destination.

3. The Salmon River

The center of Idaho is not an easy place to live. Idaho County, which includes Riggins, is the largest county by size but one of the least populated. It is cut by Highway 95—the only road that travels the whole state, linking north to south—and bordered by the Salmon River.

The Salmon heads north and west from its headwaters in the Sawtooths. Tracing it on a map, the curves of the main stem resemble a sideways question mark, or the scar I bear on my left elbow from the wire handle of a bailing pail during a water fight. Or, if you consider the river's south and middle forks, then the basin resembles something more like a cursive "m"—*m*—scrawled between Montana and Oregon, with a lengthy serif on the top left where it meets the Snake near the Washington border. Or perhaps, if you squint and let the lines blur a little and take in all the tributaries—Marsh Creek, Bear Valley Creek, the Secesh River, Camas Creek, Loon Creek, the Lemhi River and the rocky North Fork—it starts to resemble a beating, blue-veined heart.

But Idaho's heart is not really rivers, just as hearts are made not of blood but muscle. Rather, the Salmon River drainage pulses through the Idaho batholith, a crystalline granite formation up to two miles thick and estimated to be up to 100 million years old—mountain time in the truest sense. Over its lifetime, the river has etched canyons thousands of feet deep in this rock.

In one of those canyons runs the Middle Fork, where I met Charlie. It drops 4,000 feet in a hundred miles and was one of the original rivers designated as Wild and Scenic by Congress in 1968. There are no roads or fish hatcheries on the river, and its Chinook salmon run is one of the last wild runs of that species in the entire watershed. The fish first travel 800 miles from the ocean—that is, those that survive the slackwater, eight dams, and predation they encounter on the way—to the Middle Fork and its tributaries. Chinook numbers in the Middle Fork have declined precipitously since the 1950s, down from around 45,000 to 1,500. A sliver of their former population, they survive on the latter end of a spectrum between existence and extinction. Scientists think the Middle Fork's Chinook run will be gone in twenty years. In Charlie's and my lifetime.

4. Idaho history, briefly

I grew up in northern Idaho—North Idaho, they say, though when I was a kid we distinguished between *northern* and *north,* the latter having vague connotations of white supremacy and the former simply, but importantly, distinguishing us from Southern Idaho with its potato barons and campy, arid ethos of *Napoleon Dynamite.*

The feud between the two regions started when Idaho was a territory, a geopolitical liminality of sorts. Due to the economic importance of mining and transportation in the Snake and Salmon river canyons, Lewiston became Idaho Territory's capital in 1863; but agriculture had begun to boom down south, and southern Idahoans clamored to bring the capital to Boise. The territorial governor agreed and signed papers to that effect, then slipped town under the guise of going duck hunting. He would not set foot in the territory again.

Angry northern Idahoans attempted to prevent the legislative heist, but the seal and documents were taken to Boise by an armed militia and the new acting governor, who, upon the success of his mission, promptly lost the seal and drank himself to death.

When the territory became a state in 1890, the land-grant university was sited in Moscow on the Palouse prairie to appease the northerners' ire. That's where I grew up.

5. The Palouse

If Riggins is the middle of Idaho, then Moscow is the middle of northern Idaho—and I shouldn't say I "grew up" in Moscow, anyway; we lived a few miles east, on one of the abundant, rolling hills that characterize the area between the high deserts of eastern Washington and the rising forests of northern Idaho. The Palouse hills are made up of loess deposited by the great Missoula floods that westerly winds softly swept into elephantine humps. The soil—plentiful and fertile in a climate that doesn't thirst for irrigation—has mostly been converted to agriculture.

Local environmental groups calculate that only about 1 percent of the original Palouse prairie exists today. It's the most endangered ecosystem in the lower forty-eight states, according to the U.S. National Biological Service. Clumped with bunchgrass, hawthorn, and purple camas and populated by pheasants, white-tail deer, and the rare giant

Palouse earthworm, remnants of prairie are tucked here and there, often at the edges of Idaho's ponderosa or fir forests. But the bulk of the original habitat has gone over to monocultures: wheat, barley, lentils, or peas covering hills of such height and depth that the actual area, if rolled out by some cosmic rolling pin, must double the square mileage you'd calculate on a map.

As a child, I was mesmerized by the waves of hills, mossy brown with wisps of winter wheat peeking through as patches of snow slipped down their shoulders in late winter; emerald in the cloud-mottled spring sunlight; and, as summer set in in earnest, sheening green-gold in July before the sun baked them into August's golden harvest. I learned to walk the furrows of the fields so my feet didn't break the stalks and spent hours staring at the wind's cursive loops bending the barley, bringing Washington air to our Idaho land. The hills, like rivers I'd come to know, existed in constant flux: germinating, sprouting, ripening, drying, harvest, waiting.

Home was another place of betweenness, the sort that comes of being the children of parents who married young and would come to discover how little they had in common. My father introduced us to fishing and rivers and the feeling of never quite being satisfied with life; my mother embodied *hygge*—the Scandinavian notion, which is having a renaissance these days, of feeling satisfied to curl up with a book, a blanket, and a hot drink on cold, somber days. Growing up in the shadow of their disparate interests was in some ways the best of both worlds, but there was discomfort and even comedy in the betweenness: When it came to the outdoors, our mother entirely abandoned our care to our father, who, not used to feeding and clothing the three of us kids, would be surprised and irritated to find us starting out at the beginning of a backpacking trip in dingy white Keds, or barefoot on a raft because we'd grown out of our Tevas and no one had thought to get us new ones.

So, as soon as we could, Charlie and I escaped our parents and found a home on the rivers, rowing through days of sunshine and whitewater, until finally there was no more college to turn to when autumn came and relationships and careers pulled me, then him, from the river.

6. Back to the river

As humans, many of us eventually migrate into cities and suburbs. But I wonder if, like salmon, we haven't evolved beyond feeling the pull to return to wild places, even if the place we migrate to isn't one we stay in—that it's a betweenness, like the ocean for the sea-going salmon. That our journey isn't stationary, that we have to travel to wild places—rivers, feeder creeks, the ocean. I don't know why, and maybe it's not true for all of us.

Charlie's a firefighter now, and we see each other sometimes, living in the same town and dropping our kids off at the same elementary school. Neither of us gets back to the river often. But this summer, Charlie and I might find our old boss and see if we can borrow his rafts and take our families on a day trip. Riggins to Lucile. We'll float under the time-zone bridge and tell our kids about how it divides the state in half. We'll walk them to the old stone house and its nearby pit and tell them about the miners, and let them swim in the calm pools of the river where a few Chinook and sockeye still fin their way upstream. After we get off the river, we'll get huckleberry milkshakes, and by the time those are empty paper cups rattling on the floorboards, we'll stop at the White Bird Battlefield, where the Nez Perce successfully defeated the U.S. Army, buying themselves time and space, but not quite enough.

We're over the threshold now, no longer neophyte guides. We have jobs and mortgages and families and limited vacation time. But maybe leaving the river wasn't the last threshold to be crossed. Maybe life is a series of interstices: the calm water between rapids, the quiet places where one day, perhaps, our ashes will mingle with the ghosts of the fish, waiting for whatever comes next.

Hiking into the Backcountry, I Think of My Cousin

Michael Garrigan

and I wish I could swagger through this understory
like he did everyday down gray D.C. streets

and then he's here with me even though he hated bugs
and remember when we were playing mini golf

and I got so angry for missing a putt I swung my club
towards the castle and you held my shoulder

and said Let it go, Michael, it is not a big deal
and my anger left and you said *Michael*

not scolding but eye-level, firm, kind, the syllable-
break a soft crush of fireweed against my calf

and these larch are too tall and my tears dry in mule dust
and Cameron, my shoulders carry us into these woods.

Taking the Shot

Steve Oberlechner

I fumble for my cell phone as it vibrates on the plank floor of the Ethan Pond shelter, push off my quilt, rub my eyes with the backs of my dirty hands, and sit up in the dark morning. It's 3:30 a.m. I had set my alarm early, before the shapes of trees would be distinguished from the darkness around them, for one reason: I want to see a moose. Since entering Vermont, I have seen their tracks pressed in the mud, stepped in their shit when my eyes were searching the pines or squinting down on distant ponds from open ridgetops. The towering brown ungulates had become a personal white whale as I walked northbound and solo into the White Mountains of New Hampshire, but I had never risen to sit quietly, waiting and watching, before the volume of hikers might spook the local moose from the trail until the cover of darkness.

I feel for my boots and my socks and pull them on as the stranger who hiked in after dark snores on the opposite end of the lean-to. I remember my father shaking my shoulder as I lay in bed on winter Saturday mornings years before, remember tiptoeing down the hall past my sister's bedroom as she slept, our breakfasts of cereal and toast, layering up for the cold, zipping blaze-orange coats over thermals and vests, pulling on blaze-orange caps before we walked out to his truck.

I fish the Ziplock holding my digital camera from my backpack, slide my headlamp down over my sweat-stiffened bandanna, and follow its cone of light between the black silhouettes of pines, past empty tent platforms to where water laps at the boulders lying along the eastern edge of Ethan Pond. As I step over the rocks and roots and their shadows, I recall sitting shotgun, headlights sliding over the dark and empty road, rifles leaning between my knees as my father drove us toward my grandma's farm, the spear of his flashlight as we walked up the hill to our stand, careful to avoid shuffling leaves and cracking downed branches. We sat at the base of a tree and waited for dawn to light a field where deer often crossed through the cover of a small thicket.

As we sat, I passed the time watching gray squirrels leap through the treetops and the clouds that inched by overhead, loved listening to the bare branches rattle and the distant chatter of crows. When deer stepped from the thicket, my heart kicked as I pulled the rifle's stock tight into my right shoulder, steadied the barrel against the tree trunk, and sighted in through the scope where the deer stood close enough for me to see their flared nostrils and huffed breaths. My father whispered at my left to move slowly, take a deep breath, thumb off the safety, and fire when ready.

I reach the edge of Ethan Pond and sit on a large rock, its chill seeping through my nylon pants as I fold my knees to my chest and the first birds of the morning begin to cheep and trill from the trees at my back. Looking out over the empty water, I recall the days that crawled by without action as distant rifle reports rolled from the neighboring hillsides, recall the day more than a decade ago when my father stood and walked through the field to drive deer through the woods, toward me and my rifle. When a group of four doe approached the edge of the thicket, I wondered if these were the same deer I had watched through binoculars from the porch of grandma's house, the same fawns I had seen grow, their white spots fading to brown throughout the summer. When they stepped out into the field, I remembered my father's coaching, laid the crosshairs over the heart of the largest and squeezed the trigger, my shoulder absorbing the recoil as I watched the doe fall. The others stood frozen in fear, unable to see me and unsure of which way to run, and my heart sank as one lowered its snout to nudge at the doe that lay dead, trying to get it to stand. I clapped my gloved hands, sending them off in big, loping bounds before I walked into the field, whispered an apology, and unsnapped the knife from its sheath on my belt to get my hands bloody before my father crested the rise.

The following year, when the weather turned cold and the leaves browned and fell, when I stood in line at the sporting goods store with my father for our licenses, when we drove in the dark morning to grandma's farm, wipers pushing snow across the windshield, I couldn't shake the image of the nudge, the confusion and fear. As I sat with my father at our stand in the woods, I knew we wouldn't starve, that we hunted for sport, and though I recognized that our hunting helped prevent wasteful death, had seen my share of bloated bodies of deer on the shoulders of highways, I hoped that nothing would come as he stood to drive deer through the snowy woods. Minutes passed, and the woods remained still, the field empty of all save snow, and I began to relax. Suddenly, a lone doe emerged from the thicket. She stood roughly forty yards from my stand, and as she sniffed at the air, eyes fixed in my direction, I wondered if she was one of last year's herd, perhaps the deer that nudged what may have been her mother. I kept my rifle lowered across my knees, and as we stared at each other, I wondered if she recognized me, if she remembered. I rose to my feet to send her running, hoping my father wouldn't know he had chased a deer forward, but he had heard her, followed the tracks to where she stood, and lifted his arms in question. I nodded from my seat on the rock, weighing the guilt of killing against the shame of not killing. He walked back to where I sat, looked off into the trees, sighed, and said we should get back to the house, that we probably wouldn't see another today.

I don't know how much time has passed, but the sky has brightened and my thighs have numbed. I begin to wonder what I'm doing here, wasting hours I could be walking north before the temperature rises, watching the water for a moose that may never come. I suppose the answer lies in my father's disappointed sigh. I remember it as I walk, as I lie in my tent or on the floor of a shelter, as I sit on this rock at the water's edge.

I've trudged north nearly 600 miles from where I started, far from his footsteps, his shadow, trying to see myself for what I am without comparison. For almost two months, white blazes have led me farther away from the life left behind. I've adopted a new identity as I walk through states I'd never visited to new sights, new experiences. Still, each step farther north, farther from home, is another step taken in the woods, the same place my father brought me to, taught me in. The heavy backpack crushing down on my shoulders, cinched up around my shrinking waist, is not so different from the pack basket my father carries as he walks the woods and fields along his trapline at home. I chose to start walking the New England states, through the same mountains where E.J. Dailey and O.L. Butcher, whose stories my father reads on the couch each evening, once carried pack baskets, dragged sleds, maybe glimpsed moose as they checked their traplines at dawn. Just as my father laces his work boots and leaves for the strip mine each morning, arrives home tired, sore, and hungry, I wake up each morning, pull on my damp and reeking socks, lace boots over my sore and blistered feet and continue north. Each day presents a new lesson on the woods and the weather, necessity and luxury, my physical limits and the extent to which I'll make an effort to please. Each step toward Katahdin I imagine as a step closer to some middle, common ground, and from the first mammoth, heart-shaped track, the first pile of scat, I imagined presenting a photo of a giant bull moose, largest member of the deer family, with a sprawling basket of antlers, as a trophy to my father, some evidence to offer with no spillage of blood, no nudge and no guilt, that I listened and learned, could hunt if I had to.

Perhaps this summer-long hike is an effort to get back to the pleasure I felt sitting in the woods when no game approached, when I felt no pressure to kill, when there was only his company, the clouds, the crows, or the quiet. I lean from left to right, try to stretch my legs without dipping my boots into the water, take a breath and consider the trees and the birdsong, the blush of clouds before dawn, and think about how my father could have pushed me worse places than to all of this beauty.

As night gives to pale morning, I blow at mosquitos that whine and hover near my face, twitch to shake deer flies that land and pinch. I squint at a shape over the water's surface that I expect might be a heron or some loons bunched together, until the shape turns broadside and I see the slope of a moose's neck from the top of its head to the hump of its shoulders. A cow—no basket of antlers, but still a moose, the first I have ever seen in the wild. I inch the camera up from my lap, careful to avoid quick movement that might send her great legs scissoring for the shore, the cover of trees. My heart flutters faster. When I have the camera high enough to sight through the viewfinder, I center the head in the frame like I would for a kill shot, thumb at the zoom wheel to draw the moose closer, her ears flicking and water draining from her snout as I press my finger lightly over the flash, ready to capture a memento of this moose, of this thrill, of this pond in New Hampshire, and of the long, cold Saturdays spent sitting with my father, looking out on a field, talking only in whispers if we speak at all, until a dull orange smear of sunset is all that's left burning behind the black trees on the western horizon as he stands, walks downhill, and I follow.

Stand Back and Listen

Heather Kern

She stands
on a huge granite boulder,
her golden ringlets reflecting
the last of the sunlight.
The lake before her is calm.
Her body—just four years old—is so small
before the peak,
which rises up beyond the lake in
jagged rock edges.
Her young voice echoes off the cliff face,
a natural amphitheater.
She holds nothing back, hitting
every note as strong as she can.
"Hello from the other side..."
Somewhere, amongst the boulders
on the other side of the lake,
a pika meeps in applause.
Let me always remember to
stand back and listen.

Just a Couple Miles: Mountain Ultra-Running

Stephanie Eardley

As I run the ridges of my wilderness home, I remember the fragrant solitude of a morning many years ago, when my mother introduced me to the smell of elk. We were stealthy shadows searching for a glimpse of calves bedded in the aspen deadfall. I followed in my mother's prints, stretching my legs far and fast to match her stride. As we stepped into a hollow, the air became heavy with scent. "Stop!" She whispered, "Do you smell that?" I inhaled deeply, savoring the sweet redolence of musky bluebells and forget-me-nots. "That is elk."

In ecology, habitat imprinting is how the environments we surround ourselves with when we are younger are those that we gravitate to when we are older. My DNA is filled with the codes of naturalists and nomads. My ancestors rode in the steerage of ships and buried spouses and children as they pulled handcarts across the Midwest, all in search for Zion, and later battled drought and rattlesnakes in their efforts to settle the West. My great-grandpa was a rancher, my grandpa became a wildlife professor, my dad a biologist. Some of my earliest memories are of my dad teaching me scientific names for bedtime stories and pots of bobcat jaws cooking on the stove, with my parents spending hours extracting canines and placing them in little manilla envelopes to be studied by the state. Terry Tempest Williams wrote, "Each of us belongs to a particular landscape, one that informs who we are, a place that carries our history, our dreams, holds us to a moral line of behavior that transcends thought." I feel most at home next to trout streams with coyote tracks on the banks, along big game trails in aspen forests, and with pikas *huzzing* in talus fields. I'll never forget sleepless, full-moon nights as a child listening to elk bugle or the awe I felt when my mom took me on my first ten-mile hike and told me that there were people who didn't just climb mountains but ran them.

I met my first ultrarunner at eleven weeks pregnant. While regaling me with tales from her races and checking on my vitals, my obstetrician sent me home with a prescription for anti-nausea medication and a workout schedule, which she held me to. Six years later, while on a five-mile run, I met a woman who qualified for the Olympic Trials three times in the steeplechase. She introduced me to her hardcore friends who were ultrarunners, people who raced distances longer than a marathon, the most popular being 50k, 50-mile, 100-mile and even 200+miles.

Immediately I began adding more miles to my training and doing more push-ups. Two new pairs of trail shoes, a running pack, an assortment of chews, gels, *extra*-caffeinated jellybeans, and a subscription to *Trail Runner Magazine* later, I began plotting my first marathon distance trail run.

With the kids happily taken care of, my husband and I drive to the trailhead, the castle-like bluffs rising in the distance. My plan is to run to a series of prominent red cliffs surrounded by a chain of lakes fed by springs and snowdrifts year-round sitting at 12,500 feet, about thirteen miles past the wilderness boundary. Twenty miles is the longest distance I have ever traveled in one day—mostly hiking and a little running. Today, I plan to run in five hours the distance it would normally take me three or four days to travel. I try to not psych myself out. As if I were in middle school trying to fathom jogging four laps around the track, I repeat, *it's just a couple miles, just a couple miles, just an extra-long couple of miles*—a saying perfected on the wilderness trail crew I once worked on for the Forest Service, when hikers asked us *how much farther?* It didn't matter if it were a half-mile or ten, we weren't there yet, and one could always hike another two miles, so the answer was always the same—*just a couple miles*. Having signed up for my first 50k, the purpose of this run is to test my boundaries. I want to see how hard I can push myself for how far. As my husband, not being a runner, saddles his horse, I drown myself in DEET and sunscreen, strap on my pack, and ready my watch.

Trying to keep my feet dry at all costs, I leap the small spring whose banks are covered in elk and moose tracks. I hold my breath as the smell of sulfur and elk musk lingering in the air threatens to upheave my breakfast. Trail running has reignited my love of fitness from the daily grind of bribing my kids with fruit snacks and cartoons, while I run on the treadmill and behind the stroller. In the mountains there are logs to climb, rocks to propel myself off of, and streams and snowdrifts to wade through. With my experience as a runner, angler, and trail-crew member, running trails has become a natural extension for me to push my limits and enjoy the outdoors. I now have a way to travel to my favorite places and arrive back in time to be Mom. Though a part of me feels like I am cheating on my hiking boots, at this stage in my life, the stronger I am and faster I can run, the farther I can go and the more I get to see.

The trail winds in and out of the forest strewn with lupines and columbines. I run beneath a canopy of lodgepole pines. Dippers are bobbing for insects in the creek, and brook trout rise to a hatch of mayflies. We pass the rough two-track and tie-hack cabins from the early 1900s. The horse grunts and snorts, covering my back and legs in snot when I slacken my pace. I look at my watch. In almost an hour I've covered six miles. The lack of use on this trail means my feet spend a fair amount of time stumbling in ground squirrel holes and high-kneeing it over cinquefoil. I run past the boulder patch where my kids and I like to roast S'mores and Starbursts. I stride through the meadow where my baby fell asleep nursing in my arms and my little boy squealed with delight from catching fish after fish with his dad. Agilely, I cross the ramshackle bridge where mountain men of old built a check-dam to flood the valley and send their logs downriver for the railroad, and where my kids and I like to gorge ourselves on wild strawberries.

My muscles are warmed up; I smile ear to ear. Rid of encumbering backpacking gear, I am free to test my stamina and speed. While most of my schedule consists of taking care of others, my miles in the mountains are the time I invest in myself. Though my parents passed on to me their love of the outdoors, their genetic transfer also included masses of unresolved pain. By stretching my limits mentally and physically on the trails, I combat their traumatic defects by tapping into the better parts of myself, allowing myself to become a new person. As I hurdle over logs and other obstacles, I build confidence and find peace by fighting pain with pain.

Clear streams, meadows blooming in shooting stars, and subalpine fir knotted with krummholz at timberline: this is the habitat I want imprinted on my children's hearts—an environment that will enhance their natural talents while also providing them with the tools they will need to counter life's challenges. Together on these trails and along these meadows, we have watched white-tail jackrabbits turn from brown to white and bluebirds build their nests, examined porcupine quills, and lain in warm deer beds. These are the ridges where I followed them as they followed their senses in sagebrush flats and alpine meadows, captivated by rose hips and flicker feathers along the allure of big game trails. It's here that they're learning their numbers by counting rocks they throw in the streams and their mosquito bites. For my son learning the alphabet, L was for *lichen*; for my daughter, M for *mountain*.

The trail ventures into the forest. Grey jays follow, assessing me for opportunity. Time ticking, one foot after the other. At ten miles in, I am maintaining my goal of a 10- to 12-minute mile pace, keeping the intensity light. I feel the rhythm of the landscape with my pulse, my shoes striking the surface softly. I am flying. My cadence is composed of the dappled sunlight falling through the lodgepole canopy, chickaree squirrels sounding the alarm, and the knocking of elk hooves and high-pitched whistles reverberating like a wake around me. My senses are alive, operating on instinct. I have found the elusive runner's high, that hyper-focused condition scientists describe as "a state of mind where anything is possible, where we become our most productive, creative, and powerful selves." In *Silent Spring* Rachel Carson writes, "Those who contemplate the beauty of the earth find reserves of strength that will endure as long as life lasts." As I vault over a logjam, my husband gives me a thumbs-up, and we continue to climb, returning to trails and ridges layered with elk and bear tracks, where weathered signs stand as markers for those who know where to find them.

Catching glimpses of antlered bronze bodies in the forest, we trek higher, in and out of meadows with waves of flax so blue I feel I am running on water. Scurrying up the last of the switchbacks, where the cliffs rise above timberline, I am rewarded with another surge of adrenaline. While I am bushwhacking the final stretch, my husband shows his true horsemanship expertise as he weaves the fox trotter over and through the thick downfall of giant spruce trees. The higher I climb, the farther I want to go, and the more my heart is longing to see the peaks and meadows and passes that I haven't seen since I had kids. I pass the tree with the frown on the trunk where the axe-handle broke mid-swing nine years ago. To get here in three hours and forty-five minutes is an awesome feat. I have never felt stronger. In genetics there are certain genes that wait for the right stimulus to come along to be expressed. As I chopped trees off these trails, I always wondered how I'd fare as a mountain runner, and I was certain that after having kids my prime physical fitness window was over. Yet my mile times are dropping, and I am adding more distance than ever before, even placing in and winning races occasionally. Trail running has unlocked atavistic potential for me that I never knew existed. Reaching the upper lake, I jog to the deep end, find an overhanging cliff, quickly strip off my clothes before my body cools down, and jump in the icy alpine water. All I see are bubbles as I sink into the murky teal water made from glaciers of old and feel the frigid exhilaration in my legs and lungs. Surfacing, I erupt into laughter. Not giving myself a chance to shiver, I dive down two more times. The water soothes my bleeding, scratched-up muddy legs and rejuvenates me. My husband takes a few casts with his flyrod, while I inhale some calories and ready myself for the trip back down.

At mile eighteen, fatigue begins to set in, and I remind myself to pick my feet up higher to avoid faceplanting. Exhaustion hits heavy in the next three miles. I am starting to break. My legs feel like lead. I unzip a pocket to grab a watermelon chew and end up with a handful of goldfish crackers that my toddler stuffed in my pack. The Paw Patrol theme song has become an indestructible earworm. A river is flowing down the trail from the thunderstorm two days ago, but I no longer have the willpower to hop from rock to rock. Another 10k feels nauseating. I begin to doubt my abilities and to see only my flaws. As a kid, I was always told I was weak, stupid, and worthless; one of my greatest fears has always been that it's true. I know what it's like to hate your own blood, to be rejected and betrayed by those whose codes form your very existence, and to continually battle between different truths and realities. I lived life on the edge waiting for tempers to detonate, maneuvering through mind games, and playing dumb to avoid sexually explicit conversations, while trying to never be in a room alone. Growing up, I felt suffocated and trapped, so I ran. The rawness of running has often been my litmus test for reality and my source of happiness. I have no doubt that one of the reasons I fell in love with my husband was because his biceps are the size of tree trunks. Now, fourteen years of marriage, two kids, six-hundred books, and thousands of miles spent adventuring together later, here we are with him eating my extra snacks and joking about how sore his rear end is going to be from the saddle tomorrow. I am too tired to roll my eyes, so, instead, I flip him the bird.

Despite my efforts to metabolize my childhood trauma and provide the best home for my children, I know that they will still face trials and heartache. Perhaps one of the greatest gifts my experience in the mountains has unlocked for me is the primal instinct to survive, to grab another gear and keep moving. The key to training for an ultramarathon is to slowly and consistently increase stress on your structures by no more than ten percent each week. Consequently, preparing for an ultra can take years. In the same way, as we hike, fish, and explore, I lovingly accustom my children to the discomfort that comes from fatigue, rugged terrain, and inclement weather, in hopes of incrementally building the strength of their structures and minds. I hope that by habitually exposing my children to the beauty and inherent stress of the wilderness, by cultivating their confidence and nurturing their curiosity, the talents and gifts embedded within them will be kindled, and they will not be daunted by steep slopes or boulder fields, but will instead use them to propel themselves to greater heights. I hope they will remember to observe the dippers and the smell of elk the way my mother taught me to do back when we were stealthy shadows searching for a glimpse of calves bedded in the deadfall.

Twenty-four miles, 3,500 feet of incline in a little over five hours—I have never run this long or this far. I have hit the wall. Making my way around the last big meadow, I choose to focus on the memories rooted in the ground beneath my feet, instead of on my watch and my weaknesses. I jump water bars I built in between lightning strikes, stride along the boardwalk my crew and I spent hours prying and repairing in the blazing heat. With one and a half miles left and cramps from my toes to my quads, I am exhausted, but not defeated. I'll never give up. I am home. Spying a faded smiley face on a tree that I cleared with my axe years ago, I remind myself, *it's just a couple miles.* I dig deep, grab another gear, and fly.

© 2022 by Andie Thrams

Lake Melakwa Photo

Mary Ellen Talley

Ah, the lake
he dove into—impulsive youth!
Cold glass in a deep crevasse.
He shed shoes and shirt
at the top of switchbacks,
plunged past fear,
quickly exiting,
brushed back red curls,
no towel but the shivering sun,
while she sat on a gray stone
laughing

in the only remaining photograph
of that afternoon
at Lake Melakwa
where pink heather
still scatters the hillside,
Indian Paintbrush stands
beside evergreens,
and water courses
in rivulets
over puzzles of stones.

Five Hundred Miles

Andrea Lani

My 15-year-old son Milo and I are hiking along the backbone of a ridge. The land drops away on both sides to deep, green valleys. Beyond the valleys, jagged peaks rise up, red and gray dusted with green. Farther in the distance, more mountains stretch hazy and blue to the edge of the sky. We climb up sharply, heading toward a rocky knob—the high point mentioned in the guidebook, I hope. I lift one foot after the other, repeating a mantra I found in a book on walking meditation: *I have arrived. I have arrived.* Looking down, I notice the track of a mountain bike between rocks.

"What a stupid place to ride a bike," I say.

"What a stupid place to do anything," Milo replies.

We're on day 40 of a 42-day trek of the Colorado Trail, a nearly 500-mile pathway from Denver to Durango. My husband, Curry, and our 11-year-old twin sons have hiked ahead, but Milo walks behind me. He's developed blisters across the balls of both feet and strained a tendon in one ankle. To slow down and allow his body to heal, he lets me set the pace. I'm a plodder. A dawdler. I stop and take pictures, look at the view, study flowers. Having someone hike behind me makes me feel rushed, herded. But today's the first time I've walked with Milo on this hike, so I enjoy his presence at my heels.

Most mornings, Milo and his brothers set off together at a fast clip. Curry either treks ahead with them or stays behind to wait for the tent to dry. I hike alone until lunch, with one of the twins joining me in the afternoon. I rarely see Milo except in camp and at breaks. Once he sets out, he moves as if propelled by an invisible force. I once suggested he take on "The Flash" as his trail name, for his tendency to fly up three switchbacks before the rest of us have shouldered our packs. He smiled, pleased, but chose to stick with "Flaky," the name he chose for the overgrowth of dandruff caused by showering only once every week or so.

But today Milo's pace matches mine, while I move a little faster than I normally would and forego many photo opportunities. It's mid-August and autumn has already crept onto this high ridge, turning the grass gold and withering many of the wildflowers. But the Indian paintbrush still bloom in every shade of pink—rose, blush, magenta, fuchsia, coral. To keep my mind off my tiredness, I focus on the beauty of the flowers and hum the Proclaimers' song "I'm Gonna Be," a tune we listened to on the drive from Maine, the Scottish accent serenading us across the country: "I would walk 500 miles, and I would walk 500 more..."

Five-hundred miles is an awfully long distance for a teenager and pre-teens to contemplate hiking. We would have to average a little more than 12 miles a day in order to finish the hike and get home before school started. The boys had hiked no more than seven miles with full packs, but I wasn't worried about their ability to finish the trail. I pictured them racing up mountains while I wheezed and gasped, struggling to keep up, which is how it's come to pass. More than being apprehensive about the challenge of hiking, Milo was mad that he would "miss the whole summer." His friends would be hanging out having fun, and he wouldn't be there. He also wouldn't be able to work a summer job, take driver's ed, or spend long, lazy hours doing absolutely nothing.

Milo never misses an opportunity to remind me that hiking 10 or 15 miles a day through heat or rain or hail, crouching on the ground to eat cold food, or sleeping on roots and rocks is not his idea of a good time. One evening, after a day of switchbacks which seemed to take us in circles followed by a long, steep climb in icy rain, we huddled in the wet tent, slurping cold ramen noodles. I said to the boys, "It's okay if you don't love every minute of this hike. Even awesome things suck sometimes."

"Yeah," Milo replied, "and so does this."

And yet, despite the wisecracks, he's remained cheerful all summer. He's tolerated the discomforts of the trail with greater equanimity than the rest of us, has lost his temper far less often, and has hardly complained. He and his brothers have gotten along better than they ever do at home. While they've all had to grow up a bit, taking on responsibilities not expected of them in daily life—helping to set up and take down camp, collecting and treating water, staying on the correct trail—away from the pressures and influences of school, friends, and media, Milo is freed to be a kid. Each morning the boys set out together, telling stories and inventing worlds. I catch only snippets—*El Loco... Tom Lighthouse's World...Camper Bob and Camper Joe*—before they disappear around a bend in the trail. In camp, they play poker with a tiny deck of cards or invent games, like Harry Potter Trivia or naming a fish for each letter of the alphabet *(I=interesting purple jellyfish)*. Milo doesn't know it, but this time is a gift, one last summer spent being a boy, a six-week reprieve from teenagerhood, a brief pause before becoming a man.

I don't tell him this, of course. I hike on in silence, focusing on breathing, listening to Milo talk, grunting my replies. After what feels like hours of climbing, we crest the knob of land we've been aiming for only to find it's a false summit. We have to travel downhill a bit and then climb up a higher, steeper, knobbier pile of rocks. I stop to rest, too tired to think of this hilltop as anything but a dirty trick of perspective. Later it will occur to me that parenting is one long trail studded with false summits—moments when we think we've reached the peak of rapture or exasperation over our children, only to find another, higher summit beyond.

Dark clouds amass around a jagged mountain to our west, and we need to climb up and over this high point and back down to lower ground before the clouds break free of the peak and come our way. We reach the top, the actual, truly high point, and see our destination below—Taylor Lake, a turquoise gem set in red earth. I can see the gold pyramid of our tent, already pitched among the willow bushes, and my younger two sons working their way down the switchbacks. We will make it to camp before the rain.

We arrive home in Maine a week after completing our hike, two days before school starts. The boys don't want to talk about the trail. When Curry and I propose an overnight backpacking trip in early October, they mutiny. I import my photos and type up my journal notes, but I don't bring up the trail with the kids. Life returns to normal. Months pass, and then I wake up early one morning to hear Milo in the shower, blaring music, as always, but instead of his usual rap or rock, I hear a familiar Scottish voice singing, "I would walk 500 miles, and I would walk 500 more…" A few days later I pick up a package of the crackers we ate for lunch on the trail and serve them for dinner alongside soup. I hadn't intended for them to trigger memories of the hike—I'd bought them because they were on sale—but once we start breaking apart and crunching them, the kids start reminiscing.

"Can you believe we ate these every day?" Milo says.

"Can you believe this was the best food we had?" my husband replies.

"You know, if it weren't for the dirty and disgusting parts of the trail, I'd probably do it again," Milo says.

His brothers chime in:

"I would do it again if we could ride horses."

"I'd do it again if it was in Norway and I could ride a sleigh pulled by six huskies."

"Remember how we ate cold oatmeal for breakfast every morning?" Milo says. "And it was disgusting? But you had to eat it or you'd get lightheaded and have to sit down with your head between your knees an hour later?"

"Remember the wildflowers?" I say.

"I didn't really pay attention to those," Milo says.

"You didn't see all those wildflowers?"

"I saw them, but that's not really what I was interested in. I remember the mountains."

This set off a series of remember-whens: *Remember how we pooped in a hole 42 times? Remember the pika with a daisy in its mouth? Remember the herd of bighorn sheep? Remember swimming in the ice-cold lakes? Remember how I couldn't sleep in the hotels when we went to town? Remember how hard it was to get a ride when we hitchhiked?*

"You know," Milo says, "hiking the trail is a lot better in retrospect than it was when it was happening."

"A lot of things in life are like that," I say. I think, but do not add, *including parenting.* The trick—which I'm still learning—is to appreciate life while it's happening, even when you're cold or hungry or tired or sore, when your baby is crying or your kid is driving you crazy.

I look around the table at my family, crushing cracker crumbs on their placemats and laughing over memories of dirty underwear and cold couscous, and think, *I have arrived. I have arrived.*

Why We Went to the Desert

Jill Burkey

I yearned for the slick stillness
boulders hold inside their hardness,
even for the sadness of evening primrose
collapsed by an unconscious step.

I craved the quiet cold of night
so I might see myself in stars
and mirrorless canyon walls,
bathe myself in morning, evening, and sky.

I needed her eyes to feel the red of the rocks,
her small hands to skim the surface of clear Kayenta water.
I wanted her to hear the Onion Creek honesty
flowing through Entrada earth.

But most of all, I longed for her to witness
how a little creek can push back big boulders,
and how evening primrose can rise again,
how it blossoms out of night.

And When You Speak You Hear It Still

Talley V. Kayser

This desert is a space where every voice carries.

For example: sunlight takes its first, calm breath of sky . . . and the coyotes immediately nip it in the ass. *YipyowlYIPyipyowlyip!*—the light scatters wildly, and motley brushy-tailed trickster voices bound loose and fierce from rock to rock, carrying over the horizon.

YipyowlYIPyipyowlyip! The alarm has sounded. It is morning.

So wake. Blink. Rub grit from your eyes, to better admire the frazzled light limning the twists of the juniper branches above you. Stretch, the better to feel the close coze of your sleeping bag, the better to feel your body thrumming and strong and ready. Sit up. Yawn. Muss dust from your hair. Have a look around.

The desert you slept in is flat, flat, flat: an even surface of rough grit, stabbed intermittently with cactus. In the distance, a mountain range, or something like one—a long slump of tumbledown granite (technical term: quartz monzonite). It is barren and bare and intricate with cracks and divots and shears, as finely textured as TV static. If you keep staring, it'll dizzy your eyes; the range will lean away from your gaze and unwind, low-slung as a snake, under the enormous sky.

Those are the distant mountains. Nearer, there are rocks—or something like them. Towers, spires, mounds . . . the near desert swells with jumbled piles of warped and bulbous stone that *rear,* abrupt and definite, from the flat pane of the floor. As though stone creatures have burst through the bedrock to take (at last!) a breath of air. The rock piles are as fractured and dizzying as that far-off range; they tower thirty feet, fifty feet, higher. They cast synchronous shadows of astonishing length.

The geologists, in their calloused poetry, call these odd plops of rock "inselbergs." *Island mountains.*

The rocks are, quite obviously, gods. Just watch the coyote-frazzled light pant at their feet; just watch their shadows stretch in respectful silence, royal trains with a deep, deep color that has no name. The rocks are gods, and we are their prophets, and already we are moving through the light.

You're missing out. So. Unslip your legs from the sleeping bag. There's no need to change; what you were and wore yesterday, you are and wear today. Grab the boots you cast off last night and shake them out at arm's length, giving scorpions and tarantulas respectful opportunity to exit. Don your hooves, then shuffle the sleeping bag into a stuff sack. Set the bundle on your sleeping pad. Weight both with a rock. Congratulations—your room is clean.

(This despite the distinctive, twisted turd fifteen feet to your right, which was not there yesterday evening. Be glad: the coyote people have passed by in the night.)

Stand. Feel your legs desert-strong, centered; lope across the flat desert floor, skirting hazardous tufts of misnamed teddy-bear cholla, to where four people gather around a hewn picnic table. (That's me, there, the one with her feet up and her face to the sun—the one decorating her coffee with a glug of Bulleit. Cheers, and good morning!)

Shuffle over to the scuffed cooler you keep tucked in shade. What have you got?

You have an onion and some cheese—I have eggs—Maura has two bell peppers and a tomato—Keo's cooking gear is already set up and alight. The prophets will feed, and as we feed, plan the day's worship: which palms will sweat against what god's body, which hands will crimp and clutch which hunks of rock. Which breaths will circle that small bit of sky that separates us from our next movement, the next hold.

We plan the day's climbing, and the desert carries our voices. The light sneaks through the convoluted terrain, and (finding coyotes gone quiet) grows bolder. Settles. Warms.

The whole gods-and-prophets thing sounds nice, but it's bullshit.

First of all: mid-sized piles of rock make for terrible gods. (Don't they?)

Second of all: we preach but little. Sure, there's some fire and brimstone—vague sounds about climate change, fossil fuels, whether one can in good conscience bear children in this unraveling world. But really. Apocalyptic rhetoric is not our go-to.

Third of all: what god would accept us? Ragtag scruffy band of bipeds. Itinerant makeshift cretins belching and cursing and sweating our ways up and down granite (quartz monzonite) as sun blasts rock. We are riffraff. We make trouble. We make noise. We make love, or something like it, with implausible people under implausible conditions, and pick cactus needles from implausible places afterward. In short: we behave badly, in the mediocre manner of middle-class countercultural twenty-somethings, rarely mindful of the safety nets and college degrees that allow us to find sleeping in the dirt and hodgepodging our meals freeing and exotic. No prophets, we.

And yet. The nights.

Now that the day is done—now that our bodies are rocksore and worked—now that we've swilled down the hodgepodge evening meal (guarantee: it involves sweet potatoes and onions) and one-point-five beers apiece—now that the skydark swarms with stars, and the moon has started rising just south of camp, pillowing the nearest island mountain—clamber with me. Strap this guitar to your back, or tuck this harmonica in your pocket, and take that remaining half-beer in one hand, and call to the knot of lollygagging shadows round the fire that we're going up. A few always come.

We lope together to the base of the nearest inselberg, the nearest *island mountain*. Our palms are all crusted and flaked; our touch against the rock is as textured as the rock. We've grown paws, and thus roughened we move easily over the lower slabs. Moon peers into the hollows of our beer bottles, shakes its head, laughs.

Hold on. It gets steeper here. I'll give you a hand.

Reach back; help the person behind you.

See the (full) moon (fully) rise. See. See that you see, that you see as though it is daylight. See your shadow perfect against the stone, down to the hairs on your head; see your shadow climb perfectly, pressing its body against every fleck of feldspar, quartz, mica. Heave your shadow over the top, and stand on a wide convoluted platform of rock, dipping and rolling and open to the night, lit bright as any stage. Settle in as the others ascend, until our laughter cools suddenly into quiet as we look out together.

Because the desert is not spread out before us in the moonlight.

Because the moonlight, the desert, the great glowing etch and shade of the world we move through, has swallowed us.

In time, we unhitch hinges on old guitar cases. Sound flickers, flickers, catches, builds. Becomes music. Messy irregular, honest-to-gods music shaped by nothing but hands in loose rhythm and whatever ready notes follow. We laugh, we sing. Our voices are rough and raw; we are full-throated and luminously drunk; we are trouble.

But that desert carries our voices. The desert carries every voice.

And perhaps we *are* prophets, or something like them. After all, we rise with the coyotes. We walk to the rocks. We spend our days in contact, with rock and each other, our palms thick with chalk and sweat in equal measure—our palms pouring reverence and fear and anger and wonder and focus against the *quartz monzonite,* the granite-not-granite. We roll blank bedrolls under the stars, or under the shadows: shadows woven by juniper, shadows bristling with needle and frond, shadows smoother than the islands that cast them. When we wake, we shake decomposed granite from our ruffs and lope into the next day, easy with joy.

And when it comes time to leave—when November hinges open its doors to the wind—we carry the desert, too. Not only in our rough palms, in the cactus needles we pluck from improbable places, in the scuffs and scars that finely texture our skin. These smooth, disappear, fade.

But speak of the desert, and you will hear it. Rough and raw, intricate and finely textured. Quavering at the edges with coyote mornings, but centered and full as moon.

Your voice—it carries the desert.

© 2022 by Andie Thrams

Tom

Bill Simmons

The last time we talked, you were

Wanting to get away for a while.

We discussed the Pacific Crest Trail.

You got excited when I mentioned

I had been on it a few yards

While climbing Mount Whitney.

We talked about the trail going north

From Trail Crest to Yosemite,

The frozen lakes, the shadows

Of snowy peaks, the deep, deep blue sky.

We began to plan stash sites; you said

You had relatives near the trail.

Two weeks, we thought, would do us good;

Our date was sometime in June;

We were to keep in touch.

Then six months later you took the trip

Without me, a heroin overdose.

My Friend,

I wanted to tell you,

From the top of Mount Whitney

You can see Death Valley.

Bill

Whisker Lake

Brandon Hansen

There it was, the tap, the whisper of a nibble on the baked bean lanced by the thin hook, silver like polished steel. The bobber twitched, twitched, and with a wrist snap, the minnow—the pearly dace—danced in my palm. I flicked what was left of the baked bean into the water. There was a ripple, then a cloud of minnows that attacked the scent and destroyed the mirror of Whisker Lake.

I plugged the hook into the nostril of the pearly dace. I cast it deep into the lake. A trick my dad taught me. The line fell on the water as if drifting to sleep.

The fallen maple I balanced on lilted and swayed beneath my feet. Somewhere in the trees a bird made a noise I'd never heard before. I exhaled all my nervous breath when I remembered where I was.

My bobber twitched. The line grew tight, started to unspool from my reel, traveled like a spirit from my pole. This was it.

Dad's hunting knife was beneath the basswood tree, impressed into the earth an inch or so—just enough to dodge the chop of lawnmower blades, just enough for my dad to consider it lost forever. But as a barefoot, ever-wandering child, I nearly found it the hard way—stepping on its faded wooden handle rather than its rust-caked blade.

I showed it to my dad that evening, presented it on a paper towel across my hands like an artifact. His eyes widened to see it again. "Oh, huh," he said, before walking past me and sinking into the couch. Without looking back, he said, "I thought that'd be lying in my old deer blind, out at, oh…"

Whisker Lake. Named for its appearance after fires ripped through the Northwoods in the 1930s and burned the old-growth forest around its banks to pokey black stubble. Every time I heard the name, I thought of my dad's face during deer season, how fast he transformed when he didn't shave for a week, when he traveled in a loop of early light and early darkness from our house to his deer blind. Whisker Lake was four miles deep into the woods. The only trail there was the one generations of deer had punched through the brush, and even that was obscured by the fresh snow of late November. It was the only place my dad ever went that I didn't want to follow; Whisker Lake scared me.

Every time I bumped my knuckles against the rusted knife, which sat for a decade in the drawer of my desk, I thought of that lake and my dad being swallowed by that dark, whiskered mouth in the woods. I thought of that first night I was convinced Dad wouldn't come home, the first of many nights Mom would spend spinning the numbers on the dial phone, her frantic voice rising in pitch as the hours ticked on, as the house grew cold without Dad there to stoke the fire. I thought of the way she paced, started to scream at any of Dad's friends who would pick up in the dead of night as the snow fell outside, thought of how she cornered and questioned my brother and me, in our single-digit ages, as if we could know where Dad was, as if we could say anything except that we were sure he'd come home soon.

And he did. Well past midnight, when Mom had exhausted herself with worry and sat at the head of the table, shaking, asking us to stay up with her, his headlights bumbled up the snowy road. We could all only stare at the door as he walked in, beard still frosted, his gun at his side, a deer, gut-shot and chased through the night, lying dead in the trunk of the car. He stared at us, we stared at him. Something had changed.

In the decade since that night, the night I'm sure that Dad lost his knife while carving the deer as it hung from the basswood, there was the advent of the cellphone, of social media, of a thousand reasons to know where he was on any given night. But he was a ghost—sometimes drifting into the house near dawn after a night at deer camp with his friends, though he had stopped hunting long ago.

As I grew old enough to burn nights away with girls I liked, old enough to light the driveway with my headlights in the earliest hours of the day, it dawned on me that there are very few reasons to be away all night, very few things a person can be doing where they can't answer a text, can't look anyone in the eyes the next morning. I learned how it felt to be swallowed up.

But some of my late nights were only spent around bonfires, talking about everything beneath the stars and about the stars themselves with my friends, with people who were good for me. And that was all. Some nights were just that, and those nights I would lean back and stare at the sky and hope my dad, who I knew wouldn't be home, was at least only doing the same thing I was.

When I turned 20, the same age my dad was when he learned he would become a father, I had to go to Whisker Lake. Some magnetism pulled me to the deer trail, still clear through the woods. Branches and ferns snagged my shirt and shoelaces; I stepped carefully around baby maples while a can of beans and my tacklebox clanked together in my backpack. Dad's knife was secured to my belt.

Before the trip, I had restored the knife. I dipped the blade in vinegar, and after a few days, an amazing amount of foul-smelling crud sloughed off. I sanded the handle and the blade and blew the shiny dust into the yard. I stained the handle with the only wood stain I could find in our basement. It shocked me when I realized it was the same color as the trim around our windows, which I remember my mom and dad staining together when I was only five. Then, the day of the trip, I polished the blade until I could see myself in it, and reflect.

Despite the August heat, a chill ran through me when I saw Whisker Lake. I sat down on a fallen tree, opened my can of beans, and began to eat while I stared at the rippling water.

I knew that somewhere in the lake's perimeter I might find my dad's old hunting blind. But I hoped it was lost to time. Leaves rustled around me, and even if I was an adult now, a familiar fear shook me to think it could be the ghost of my dad with his dark beard, his silent manner, his mind cooking up whatever it was that ended those routine days of his presence in the daylight, the days when he seemed to have energy for us.

Time passed strangely at Whisker Lake. I poked around the loose bark of fallen trees with dad's knife, hoping to find a grub or worm to use as bait. I never did take up hunting, but Dad and I used to fish together as often as we shared meals. He never did say anything about fishing in Whisker Lake, though, as if there was some secret in its depths he didn't want me to see.

Evening snuck up on me, and with no bugs in sight, I turned to the can of beans. I had to catch something. I had to make something interesting enough happen that I could tell my dad about it the next time I saw him; I had to find a way to talk about Whisker Lake.

And this was it. I set the hook, felt the writhing life of whatever attacked the minnow run through the pole. I was breathless as I maneuvered the fish around the lily pads, the marsh grasses. I couldn't fail. I had to know what was in Whisker Lake, what was at the end of the line.

When the fish grew tired, I knelt down on the floating log and scooped it from the water.

A bigger minnow. With teeth. A pearly dace, as long and bright as a hunting knife.

Secret Season

Maeve McKenna

In this leafless woodland, I have come
to walk into my father's death.
Trees connive, latch their fibrous anchors

around the soles of my wet shoes, ignite
trip-wires. Ask nothing—
it is less than nothing. I cannot name loss,

so I will call it my secret season.
My father, tossed inside the winter of a coffin,
withered, offered beneath varnished dead-wood

to high altars of summer beliefs. The path thins,
disguised by impacted leaves, feet skimming
at the edges of my sorrow, pressed

to the route I must explore. I have yet to free
my body of this union. Still, the coiled heron swoops
in spring—fanned wings

I could quietly rest on—and seaweed swallows
without restraint, bubbling under
the incoming tide.

Not the Moon

Marybeth Holleman

We hike up to Blueberry Hill while the sky behind us turns a deeper orange, long sunset of January gilding our northern city far below us. Dry snow squeaks under my boots, and my husband behind me clears his throat. But when we stop, I hear what has caused my dog to stand still as stone and perk up her ears: ravens winging to roost, wings carving cold air into a lullaby. *Hush, hush, hush,* they sing, dark sickles passing above us. Orange deepens to red and melts skyline behind us as we round the corner to face jagged peaks from which we think the moon will rise. We sit on snow with backs to rock. Blue sky, purple sky, deep sky. Blue snow, purple snow, deep snow. Ravens call from we know not where, then one strokes sky overhead and is joined by the two calling, perched on the opposite mountainside, camouflaged by rocks sheering from white snow. As if two were waiting for the third, they now all head up-valley single file. I am watching last light glance a curve of white mountain against powder-blue dusk when my husband says, *There.* Just over a smooth lip in the craggy ridge, a line shines silver and grows as quickly as sunrise at the equator and not moonrise near the pole. I sit stock still, snow cold seeping up, and try to feel how it is not the moon lifting up into view but us, this Earth, that is slowly spinning. For a moment, for a half-moment, I do sense that I am turning, enough to grow dizzy and touch brief fear, like cloud wisp, of falling off, away, into stars. It's too much, the rolling of our home orb, only invisible gravity holding us here, and so we call this moon*rise*; we give moon all credit for this brilliance slipping up, over the ridge, oval stretching to complete circle of light. We say the moon is full though it is always full and only its orientation to the sun changes. We say the sun sinks, and slides, scraping the horizon red. We say ravens winging to roost do not have thought or language like ours and so, though it seems like two were calling the third, we second-guess it, spinning ourselves around again. We say whatever works to keep the ground beneath our feet solid, this boulder pressing my shoulder blades unmoving, even as we twirl like snowflakes, like motes of moonshine, giddy in the light.

Migration

Dick Anderson

The spirit of the caribou permeates
the night-shroud of the Jade Mountains
where I make my camp.

It is reflected in the moon trail
over the waters of the Kobuk.

I have come to this hallowed ground
as did our ancestors
twelve thousand years before.

Not to hunt,
though hunters still come
and leave the heads of their prey as gifts
for the ravens.

I have come to witness,
to commune,
to be transformed.

Throughout the late arctic evening,
under the star-struck sky,
I follow endless tracks along rusty sands.

Returning,
I gaze across the ghostly river,
searching the shadows.

I sleep in my tent,
earful of the night.

I wake to thundering splashes
announcing the first crossing of the day.

After their frantic dash,
the Kobuk now behind them,
the caribou gather.

Stately statues,
they eye me curiously,

then turn as one to continue their long migration.

Narrow Trail to the Western Pass
—a short haibun, with a deep bow to Master Bashõ

Christopher Norment

> *slipping on my pack*
> *adjusting straps*
> *how many mornings?*

From road's end I climbed through large swaths of forest burned during the Crescent Fire, which blew up during the summer of 2018. Yet in open places luxuriant growth of fireweed, buckbrush, serviceberry and snowberry, ferns rising from the ashes, a garden among charred logs. . . Thought of the firefighters who worked the burn and of course my son, hundreds of miles to the east and fighting other fires. Felt surprisingly weak on the first section of the trail, only two easy rising miles. Why so, after a day of rest, following a lovely 80-minute trail run, and before that a fast 12-mile hike? Discouraging, this general malaise—just sixty-seven!

> *tired and dragging*
> *old man labors on*
> *young runners race by*

Reached the trail junction—one path leading northwest to Copper Pass, the other west toward Twisp Pass. Took a break by the plunging creek, deep in the soft cool shade. Water and food, plus thoughts of my hike here last summer with Jamie and Ralph. Felt better after the break and so walked steadily toward Twisp Pass. Shortly after leaving my rest spot, I passed through a stand of beetle-killed lodgepoles, which made me think of friends and family long since gone—something solemn about the dead trees, even though the air was full of birds.

> *beetle-killed pines—*
> *flycatcher calls*
> *drifting through*

Then on to Twisp Pass, across rocky benches and drying meadows, the trail high above the South Fork of the Twisp River, alpine cirques cradled by the far granite ridge. At my feet a riot of flowers—phlox, lupine, spring beauty, stonecrop, several species of buckwheat, paintbrush, larkspur in wet places, on and on. Left the trail to Dagger Lake and climbed to where Liza, Martin, and I camped so many years ago—my son 11, my daughter 15. It was a difficult hike for Martin and we coaxed him up the trail with M & M's, while Liza cruised the pass. Then came a lovely day, wandering high country meadows just melting out from winter. Now Liza is so far away from me. Once again the pleasant mountain memories, though now laced with sadness.

> on the empty pass
> where we camped among the firs—
> lost to one child

After lunch I laid my grief aside, shouldered my pack, and walked on, north and west along a rising traverse through sun-struck glades and deep-shadow woods. I pitched my tent in the basin below Stiletto Lake, at the edge of a rock-strewn meadow full of flowers and flies, marmots and pikas. I thought about going on, but was worried about finding water farther out the ridge. So I threw on my headnet, long pants, and windbreaker and sought shade beneath some scraggly alpine larch. Cradled in heather, I waited out the deerflies and mosquitoes. To the north an alcove full of fireweed, water spilling down over bare gray granite.

After dinner I meandered through the meadow, seeking wildflowers and making my habitual lists, savoring the stillness, the dying day, Twisp Mountain laved in late light. Slept well and woke early, relishing the cool and quiet air, warm in my bag, considering the coming day.

> cup of tea at dawn
> cold water
> over cold rock

Wandered high, headed west. Good views of Twisp Mountain, Bowan, McGregor with its brilliant, crisp snowfields, Bonanza. Thought of my climb up the southeast ridge with Paul all those years ago—so difficult to let youth (only thirty-three then) rest easily, memory winnowed by nostalgia.

> hard to let go—
> the narrow ridge
> one pack, one rope

And west beyond Bridge Creek, Goode and Dome rising up, partly obscured by a thickening, smoky haze. Other climbs. Chanting Snyder's "Mid-August at Sourdough Mountain Lookout" to myself, a small and lovely poem that has stuck with me across all these years:

> "Down valley a smoke haze
> Three days heat, after five days rain. . ."

I, too, had the smoke haze, and what follows in the poem: flies, snow-water, friends far away, forgotten words, the high still air. . . and close by, rock-gardens of stonecrop, spring beauty, groundsel. Golden-mantled ground squirrels and chipmunks, mountain chickadees and dark-eyed juncos among the larches, small snow-melt ponds dried and gone to mud, ringed by sedge and alpine flowers. A decent breeze and repellent kept the mosquitoes at bay, the air to the south shining. Peace in my time.

After exploring Stiletto Lake, I broke camp and wandered back toward Twisp Pass, botanizing along the way, entranced by a species of lousewort, *Pedicularis racemosa*—a cluster of small, light purple to whitish flowers, each a tiny bird's beak, growing in a lush meadow with groundsel, lupine, and paintbrush. It put me in a good mood—the delicately curled corollas, how *racemosa* called to mind other *Pedicularis* species *(labradorica, lapponica)* in other beautiful places, a taxonomy of desire.

Falling away, then, back into the Twisp River drainage, the same trail different on the descent. (Thoughts of Heraclitus, something about never stepping twice upon the same path.) Clouds of small blue butterflies, subalpine gardens, smell of horse shit in the warm sun, easy going on the downhill slide.

> *hot dusty trail*
> *butterflies on fresh dung*
> *seek what small pleasure?*

Stopped again near the Twisp Pass/Copper Pass trail junction, where my friends and I camped last year. Then as now, quiet and peaceful; beneath the trees a cool and pleasant place for lunch after the sweaty descent. The stream less boisterous than last June, the alders leafed out and with fresh green catkins, nodding over the water. For years I have thought of this stream as "Ouzel River," and as I rested by the water one landed ten yards away and began foraging—plunging its head beneath the water, nabbing bits of food, bobbing through its curious dipper-dance. Bathed in the sound of falling water, my shoes off and feet soaking in the stream, I might have drifted off, but the determined attention of the deer flies made it hard to relax—dipterans (or rather my reaction to them) as metaphor for too much of my life.

> *last year camped with friends*
> *next to Ouzel River*
> *this summer, flies*

The last two miles were easy, pleasant. A puff of dust with each footfall, through fern-gardens and burnt-over lands. Thoughts of an IPA at the local pub, a shower. Hoping for renewed energy and always that bittersweet feeling at trail's end. . . Slower now, I know, but happy that I still can do this.

> *icy pint*
> *again that dream*
> *empty mountain trail*

Looking forward, looking back.

Author's Note: Thanks to Paul Hendricks for his help with several of the haiku in "Narrow Trail to the Western Pass."

Back to Hogcamp

David Staudt

You don't care the U. S. Forest Road's out,
leave car, strap pack on, hike with banging chest
the sand road twisting up to Hogcamp Gap.

Past the sun-cracked wooden cattle stile,
you're gladdened the old pasture there you knew
twenty years ago hard-grazed to scrabble

is meadow soft enough to walk in socks.
You lie in a good tent flapping in rain
on a pallet of switchgrass and cat's-ear,

cradled in muscles of sugar maple root,
while white gusts rounding the mountaintop
walk the rain down from Salt Log shelter.

Fifty-nine, no family, your life has stopped
making new stories. There are only these
places you knew you'd come back to once

you stopped needing reasons. You stay as long
as they let. Appalachian Trail thru-hikers,
hauling since dawn, wonder you haven't decamped.

Where you're heading, the other direction,
another five-hundred-foot climb under firs,
a white-blazed wooden post marks sky. Beyond,

all high Shenandoah's overlapping blues
fade to the color of rain beyond the James.
The mile-long high grass bald on this summit

wind first seeded in the Pleistocene,
the meadow cleared summers by mastodons.
Its mammoth back of hairgrass still humps

west to the riding blue bellies of clouds.
Sedges toss chromed by millennial sun.
Rhyolite outcrops, still warm, still fit your back.

Hungry for an altitude out of self,
you've come back dumbly like the mastodons,
centuries of bison, final summer hogs,

last of your kind, secure while it remains.
When the last day-hikers drain from the trails,
you pitch your tent in ripening light

downslope in encroaching willow and oaks,
your campfire and the weight of your footsteps
holding back forest another few days.

Hiking Through History: Trailless on the Steppe

Tjibbe Kampstra

For several days I had scoured the internet, seeking clues about a trail through the Bogd Khan Mountains—from Manzushir Monastery to Ulaanbaatar, the capital city of Mongolia. Unable to find an iota of information, I resorted to studying satellite maps. Staring endlessly at grainy images of forests and grasslands did not provide additional insights. Instead, I accepted the inevitable uncertainty that results from such an endeavor and decided to just go for it, hoping for the best.

Early in the morning, I walked from my apartment to the State Department Store, a remnant of Communist times, where I met my driver. My colleague had arranged for him to drive me fifty kilometers from Ulaanbaatar to Manzushir, around the imposing Bogd Khan Mountains. Though it was already May, the temperature was a brisk 37 degrees Fahrenheit. For over an hour, I sat silently next to my driver, unable to even communicate at an elementary level. After passing the last town, Zuunmod, we turned left onto an unpaved road. Over the years, cars had carved their presence in the landscape, leaving old tire tracks between the dry grass-covered sloping hills. A cloud of dust followed us as we advanced gently. The car inched delicately forward across the decrepit wooden bridge, suggesting that one erratic maneuver could disintegrate the entire structure. My driver's Toyota Prius seemed feeble as it jolted from side to side, encountering a rocky stretch. Finally, the vehicle came to a screeching halt at the end of the dirt road at the foot of the mountains.

I thanked my driver and stepped out of the car. Seeing the monastery in the distance, I checked my compass and started my journey north, back to Ulaanbaatar. Hoisting my backpack—containing only essentials such as food and water—over my shoulder, I began ascending the gently sloping path to Manzushir. I turned my head to take a final look at my driver and waved him goodbye. He must have wondered why I wanted to be abandoned in such a remote area.

Manzushir Monastery stood monumental, overseeing the large valley covered by dry grass. Tiny green pine trees topped the flowing hills, stretching as far as the eye can see, forming an alluring yet ominous contrast with the dark grey clouds. Rifts in the clouds exposed specks of blue sky, through which bright rays of sunlight transformed the stale brown grass to luminous gold. The main structure was protected by a wooden wall; while it was once covered in fresh white paint, it was now revealing much of its natural light-brown texture. The yellow roof contrasted starkly with the faded red paint on the sides of the building, giving it a dilapidated ambience.

The ruins of the original monastery at the foot of the Bogd Khan mountains, the start of my journey to Ulaanbaatar.

While historic, this is not the original structure of the monastery. This replica was rebuilt after the 1990 Democratic Revolution. Manzushir Monastery was first established in the early eighteenth century. It expanded over time and became one of the region's most important monastic centers with twenty temples and hundreds of Buddhist monks. In the 1930s, Communism was on the rise in Mongolia. Supported by the Soviet Union, thousands of Buddhist monks were purged, and hundreds of monasteries were ravaged. Standing on the site of great injustice, I could not help but wonder about the effects of Soviet influence. It has forever changed the trajectory of Mongolia: most of the country managed to defend its independence against China while the economy grew rapidly, powered by investments and financial aid. Sadly, the country also lost some of its culture, as people were forced to urbanize and leave their nomadic heritage behind. It is hard to imagine what this magnificent country would be like without the forced urbanization.

I resumed my journey, further ascending the increasingly steep slope. An *ovoo* marked my first peak. These are shamanistic cairns made from large piles of rock, repositories of offerings for local spirits often adorned with ceremonial blue scarfs or *khadag*. Upon arriving, it is customary to walk around them three times clockwise and make a wish or offering. This offering can be money, strands of horsehair, a blue scarf, or simply another rock. It is said that every rock wants to grow up to be on top of the mountain; thus, putting a stone on top of the ovoo makes nature happy. Upon completing the walkaround, I delicately placed a stone on the pile and wished for a safe journey.

This relatively simple *ovoo* marked the first peak on my journey. There are much more complex versions closer to populated areas.

Beyond the *ovoo,* a plateau stretched out several hundred yards. The treeless landscape of the plateau made sheltering hopeless; heavy winds hammered me relentlessly. Cow manure implied that I was still near herders, and by extension, civilization. Far in the distance, peak after peak unveiled a challenging journey ahead. I descended into a dense forest, and all turned quiet. The stillness was hauntingly beautiful. No humans. No birds. Just silence. The eerie calm was abruptly interrupted by the wind blowing two oblique trees against one another, producing a creepy, squeaking sound. Aged trees, possibly felled in a storm, lay littered across the forest, forming a natural obstacle course. The scent of rotting wood was pleasant in comparison to the unavoidable, putrid smell of coal that blankets Ulaanbaatar until the cold spring gives way to the summer. Passing tree after tree, stepping over large rocks and fallen trees, I made my way forward, descending towards a valley.

I felt tiny and insignificant hiking through this mighty forest as I absorbed my unique surroundings. The Bogd Khan Mountains, a UNESCO World Heritage Site, are known as a sacred place. The gently sloping mountains cover an area of 260 square miles and harbor an abundance of wildlife. Its many peaks seem equally tall and contain several hidden summits. For many years, religious ceremonies have been conducted on its highest peak, Tsetsee Gun. Its protected status for the past 300 years means it was the first national park in the world. As I exited the thick forest, the sound of trickling water broke the seemingly endless silence. On the edge of the forest, a thick sheet of ice melted gradually in the shade. Carefully placing one foot in front of the other, I crossed the slippery block, hoping that it would be strong enough to hold my weight.

The thick forest and scattered rocks made it difficult to navigate the mountains. Yet the rugged terrain has an undeniable beauty.

I ascended a treeless peak covered in high grass to gain a better vantage point. Strong winds blew snow horizontally across the top, evidence of the unpredictable weather in late spring. I continued to climb and descend small peaks for hours and hours, seeking the path of least resistance, flowing with the landscape. My surroundings alternated between dense forests on gentle slopes and valleys covered in high grass: typical open spaces of a steppe landscape. I avoided the treeless scree-covered peaks, despite my curiosity about the view. Given the unknown length of this hike, I had to conserve my energy as much as possible. When exhaustion started to set in, I wondered if I had bitten off more than I could chew. The only option was to keep going, as no one would be waiting for me back at the monastery. When large boulders blocked my path from top to bottom, I diverted my path and descended a very steep slope. I clung to thin trees as I carefully made my way down.

Unsure of how long this journey would take me, I kept breaks to a minimum, occasionally snacking on nuts, dried fruit, and meat. I felt the pressure to be out of the mountains before sunset; failing to do so would be disastrous, as temperatures could plummet and navigating would be difficult.

The valley showed no signs of civilization; high grass and the lack of excrement marked the absence of livestock. My cellphone had lost coverage many hours ago; there are no emergency-exit opportunities in this isolated landscape. I was startled by the unexpected bark of a dog far in the distance. Having not heard a sound for many hours, this one made me unusually uneasy. Before I could take another step, a massive wild boar bolted out of the bushes. I stood frozen to the ground in a state of utter exhaustion; I was incapable of defending myself as it charged in my direction. Sturdy hooves under its robust body, which was covered in a coarse coat of thick black and rusty red hairs, produced a thundering sound. Long sharp tusks protruded from its mouth. Its adorable blunt snout only made it marginally less terrifying. I sighed with relief as it dashed by me. The relief quickly gave way to the realization that there might be others. Without anything to defend me, I picked up a large rock and carried it with me for the next hour, constantly scanning my surroundings for other wild animals.

The rough landscape of the Bogd Khan mountains is shaped by strong winds and freezing temperatures. Sadly, irresponsible camping has marred the scenery, due to accidental forest fires.

Navigating a rough landscape covered in high grass without the ability to go on autopilot proved to be much more exhausting than I had expected. A scree-covered peak suggested I was close to my destination. As I stood at the top, the bright orange sun peeked through the clouds while it drifted towards the horizon. I looked back at my journey, a little over 16 miles according to my watch. Seemingly endless peaks and valleys stretched out as far as the eye could see. It was breathtaking and humbling. Nature in this country is pristine, and adventures like these are unique. My mind wandered. What would the future hold for Mongolia? As the government is attempting to combat dire poverty, the country hands out exploration licenses to expand mining operations. Simultaneously, there is a push to spur development that will help to attract tourists. While this development will help alleviate poverty, a shift that is desperately needed, it will undoubtedly have an increased effect on the habitat of many species. Over the past decades, many rivers have already disappeared, and many species have been pushed to the brink of extinction. Can a country with weak governance, grappling with the challenges of economic development, ensure that its natural environment does not pay the price? Will Mongolia be able to protect its nature, or will the pressure to excavate and sell the country's natural riches be too great to resist?

Taken by drone from a viewpoint at 2,200 meters on the north side of the Bogd Khan mountains, close to where I ended my journey. Facing south, small peaks extend as far as the eye can see.

at home in the wild heart

Matthew Lovegrove

at home in the
        wild heart
    of the Coast Mountains,
            the sun shears off
                    castellated peaks,
            casting shadows
    on the valley floor.

        at the end
                of summer,
        sky-hung lakes
                fall dark
            inside an
        apron of talus.

    the occasional rattle
                of rockfall
                pierces the silence
        so deeply
        that stars bleed out
                even brighter.

        we breathe in
                this beauty
            from the peaks
        that we carry
            with us this,
    and every night.

        a warm breeze
            the last of its kind
        before winter —

        the beating of the
        tent flap
    is the heartbeat
            I dream to.

Marlatt's Brood XIX

Grant Deam

Thirteen years ago, I was working as a graduate assistant for a biologist and wondering what the point of it all was. He was fascinated with cicadas, taught entire courses on them at the university. My duties primarily consisted of tracking the large, winged insects as they surfaced, typically after a warm rain. I photographed them molting, their alien bodies materializing out of plastic-like orange exoskeletons, mapped the trees from which their choruses hummed, noted green or black body color to differentiate between annual and periodical broods.

Professor Holmes' conviction that there was much to be gained from these wax-winged creatures fueled his passion, made him believe they could teach us humans something about engineering ingenuity, provide some crucial bit of information to help mitigate our impending climate crisis. Where many viewed the large, juicy bugs as a menace or plague, the professor saw something quite different. He was convinced that out of more than 3,400 species these cicadas were special. Sure, he romanticized the males' song, the incessant throb that attracts females or alerts others of predators. But what he was really interested in were their nanopillars, these cone-like structures on their wings, and this specific brood had glorious nanopillars.

Looking up from a lab microscope one afternoon, he exclaimed, "They build these things out of nothing!" He pushed his swivel chair back from the table. "Secretion of a compound and POOF—a wing that can kill bacteria. Repel water. Self-clean!"

But I was also aware that others, concerned about the cicada's buzz causing hearing damage, weren't so enthusiastic about them. Personally, I didn't doubt the insect's ability to harm, either through their whirs that began in the afternoon and lasted until nightfall or by their sheer appearance.

"These locusts are so gross," my parents would say, picking their bodies off the cars or backyard shed roof. That was the summer when Marlatt's Brood XIX had last surfaced, when I was nine, a summer full of pool parties and Wiffle Ball games, nights of flashlight tag and pickup basketball below the glow of the cul-de-sac streetlights, most of it to the soundtrack of the insects' hum. If you've ever been trapped in a small room with a cicada, you know it's unsettling. The *thunk* of their bodies hitting the walls and furniture or the pattering of their wings on hardwood gives a person goosebumps. For the less tolerant, it takes more than a few *thwacks* with a flip-flop to kill this insect, which is sadly how some dealt with them.

During my time as his assistant, I never told Professor Holmes that I had observed this brood before, this combination of both *Magicada neotredemcim* and *Magicada tredemic.* Never told him how they flew around our cul-de-sac and backyards. Into the bright fluorescence of open garages at night in an almost drunken manner, zig-zagging here and there. Perhaps I was ashamed that I had witnessed countless members of the brood crushed by Wiffle Ball bat smashes. The last time we played Wiffle Ball was at night. A cicada, probably near the end of its life, came fluttering down from the tree next to the streetlight. It twirled, translucent wings turning burnt orange as they caught the glow.

Had I known then what I know now, I never would have swung. Maybe I would have even stopped my friends. Maybe it wouldn't have made a difference. But I was just a kid, in a rush to grow up, to stop playing make believe. Now, that saying haunts me: *At some point in your childhood, you and your friends went outside to play together for the last time, and nobody knew it.*

Toward the end of summer, when my time in the lab was almost finished, the professor grew increasingly energetic, almost manic. Disheveled hair. Coffee-stained white coat. Fingerprints clouding up his glasses. He was close to a breakthrough. Analysis of recent nanopillar slides had led to new theories around their application to solar panel design, a better, more natural way to generate energy.

I did not share his excitement. Instead, I felt I had more life to figure out than I did at the start of my assistantship. I needed to determine my next move, the next chapter, and the passions of others could not cloud this plotting. I didn't care about our species' collective depletion of resources.

Despite his intense focus on the research, Holmes noticed my diminished interest, how I was retreating inward. On my last morning, he asked, "Did you know that some cicadas are in fact zombies?"

It was the only time all summer that he had my full attention. "As in alive but dead?"

The professor removed his still-smudged glasses, indents bookending the bridge of his nose. "Precisely. Massospora, a certain kind of fungus, will enter the cicada's body and take over, eventually controlling everything but the wings."

I pictured these parasites infecting the defenseless bugs as they slowly dug their way to the surface. Had this notion of always striving toward an undefined future, of fulfilling some greater, innate, unnamed purpose, become my parasite? Had this self-induced caging of thoughts that wouldn't allow me to turn back or live in the moment morphed into some type of mind fungus? "Why not the wings?"

"Because for all their cleverness, Massospora do not know how to fly. The infected cicada will still surface, still take off even though it is not truly in command of its faculties."

"And continue living?"

"And continue living."

After two more years of graduate school, I landed a job at a big downtown firm, but after working this job for a decade, getting used to the grind, and making a little money, I got bored and started to feel something. A shift. A fear.

Nights after taking the subway home to my apartment overlooking the park become restless. I lay awake, scrolling through websites like CicadaMania.com. It was through this minimal research that I learned some cicadas will take back control. They'll learn to tame the parasite inside them. Live harmoniously. Share nutrients. Share a brain. Certainly, Professor Holmes had been aware of these facts but had decided not to tell me. Instead he explained how the lifecycle of these creatures is quite a strange phenomenon. They hatch, spend weeks inside the slit of a tree branch before falling to the earth and tunneling, tunneling, tunneling. Professor Holmes stated that for all the research he and others have done, we still know very little about the 13 years spent underground by Marlatt's Brood XIX.

"Sure, we know they latch onto roots," he said one morning out near the greenhouses. "We know that while underground they suck the sap from these roots, and yet rarely kill the tree itself." As he stared at me to impart this knowledge, eyes bloodshot and tired and somehow full of life, it felt as if he were looking through me. He was lost in his pursuit. In discovering. "But they can only do that for so many hours of the day."

I failed to appreciate his work at the time. Couldn't get over the fact that these ugly, fat little things spent several years underground, sucking the life out of the dirt, and for what? A couple weeks of sex and death? There has to be more to it, right?

Now, I hear them humming again. In the coming weeks, with the warm rain, millions more will surface. Again, they will blink their jewel-like eyes, flex their waxy nanopillars, a chorus buzzing louder and louder, reminding me to crawl out of the dirt.

at eagle lake in the early fall

George Perreault

i leave ponderosa and fir to walk out
into grass knee-high with summer but
bent low as october nears,
                              two boats
drift-fishing for rainbow, the lake calling
blue as an archangel
                              but not more than
this field reefed with whitened shells,
remnants of an earlier edge, thick as galaxies
among autumn's scattered growth,
                              these
harvested mullein and thistle-clasps now
bleached into final glory, whole cathedrals
of chamisa, stems only green at distance, raising
their blazoned candelabras gold and linen
coalesced to the color of worship,
                              marsh hawks
gliding owl-faced and trailing white
                              as i ask
for years in fields more desolate than fallow,
the slow rise and fall of waters, a dance less
stately than mountains but still fire and
flood the blink of an eye,
                              ask to marry
this morning's headlines: human remains
a missing woman found:
                              ask to lie in paling
sun and be the everything else,
                              let something
eat the unfound me:
                              beetle, fox, or crow,
the air and wind itself,
                              the hungry anything:
and let me be then

                              earth at last.

Lessons in Survival

Paula MacKay

Nine knee-jarring miles from the North Cascades Highway, I try to picture a scenario that doesn't end in disaster. "ONE at a TIME on BRIDGE," reads the foreboding sign. Although the letters are neatly carved, their subtext is much messier. *You don't want to lose everyone in your party.*

I size up the span to the other side. The crossing is about as wide as a Seattle street, but we're a very long way from the tameness of the city. The bridge has no guardrails—only shoulder-height cables to guide wobbly hikers. Twelve feet below, a relentless rush of rapids thunders through bone-breaking boulders. Most alarming of all, the narrow slats are too far apart for our husky mix, Alder, whose paws are sure to slip through the spaces between.

Maybe Robert can strap Alder to his chest like he's carrying a baby, leaving hands free to grip the cables while they traverse the raging creek. But what if Alder spooks in the middle and tosses them both over the edge? I'll be standing here helpless while a tumble of arms, legs, and tail brings my family trio to an end. I'll also see my research partner of twenty years disappear into the froth.

We've just launched our field season monitoring wolverines— secretive, solitary carnivores who are clawing their way back to Washington after being killed off by people a century ago. I've sighted a single wolverine in our countless trips through the high country, a glimpse of sinuous grace on an avalanche slope. Today, we're headed to a motion-triggered camera deployed by colleagues last fall; cameras are the hidden eyes of science when animals have the winter forest to themselves. If we turn around now, we might miss rare photos of rewilding in action.

My best friends poised next to me on the rocks, I'm caught in a three-way tug between anxiety, love, and looming loss. Like clockwork, the dark memory lights up in my monkey mind. Bathroom door shut tight, my mother unbuttons her blouse to expose the raw, pink tissue where her left breast had been. I've hounded her to show me—I'm a ten-year-old tomboy, after all, so cuts and bruises are a matter of great pride. But the wound on my mother's chest fills me with dread. Some sinister force has consumed her flesh, and neither she nor I will ever be safe again.

"What if I clip into the cable with a carabiner and rope?" my husband asks, eager as always for a physical challenge. He holds up the cord we brought along to hang food.

Alder shifts nervously between us, rump resting on my boot. "Even if that catches you," I reply, "your weight will tip the bridge while you're dangling in the air. I'll have no way to save you without falling myself."

Robert's sun-damaged lips soften as he restuffs his pack. I know he'll acquiesce—he hates to trigger my worries—but I want him to embrace our decision as mutual so I don't feel like I'm the quitter. Nobody likes a quitter, my mother used to say.

"Take off your sunglasses, look me in the eyes, and tell me what you'd do if it were up to you," I plead.

Robert plucks the frames from his face to reveal his orbs of blue ice. "If it were me," he answers slowly, "I might take the risk." His unspoken words hang like heavy mist in the alpine air. "But I'm not the one who would have to call in the helicopter."

Helicopter. The word kicks up images I don't want to reinhabit: ambulance, hospital, the unspeakable void. Yes, the worst possible scenario *can* happen; if I learned anything as a child, it's that worrying is not a superpower. But unlike that scared little girl, I can make empowering choices—because my terminally-ill mother taught me how to be a survivor. And sometimes that means knowing when to surrender.

We step away from the bridge and haul five days' worth of meals and gear all the way back to our car. In the midnight blackness, the highway belongs to the wild. Mule deer shine in our headlights. A mountain goat wanders the shoulder like a ghost.

The Wheel

Peter Anderson

Since the cranes appear in late February and are gone by the time the vultures arrive in early April, since the aspens will leaf out a few weeks later and the warblers will find shelter there, since the wind will blow till most of the snow is gone from the high peaks and the meadowlarks offer their lilting serenade from valley cottonwoods, since the creeks will rise as the sun tracks north toward its solstice, since the swallows and nighthawks will swoop through the end-of-day sky chasing the smaller winged ones, since a river of bats will emerge every evening from the old mine up north to do the same, since the bluebirds will be hatching and minding their young ones, since thunderheads trailing veils of rain will drift across the valley on July afternoons, since the blue columbines will grace the edges of talus slopes and boulder fields up high, since valley meadows will go yellow with black-eyed Susans and purple with the blooms of asters and beeplants, since the sun will settle into a more southerly path, rendering the light a little softer on August afternoons, since the hummingbirds will leave on their impossibly long flight to Central and South America, since the hermit thrush will add a few more ethereal refrains in the last light of an Indian summer evening before joining the great wave of songbirds headed south, since only the regulars—nuthatches, juncos, chickadees, and jays among them—will fill this hillside with their presence while the dippers flash through the riffles of the creeks in the canyons, since the elk will be bugling for their mates as the snowline descends from the high ridges, since whirling showers of yellow aspen leaves will be released to the wind, since the bears will forage through remnant patches of rosehips and chokecherries, since southbound cranes will fly out of low autumn clouds, pausing for a few weeks to glean the grain left behind from valley harvests, since the first flurries of snow will drift across the lower reaches of the higher elevations where the ptarmigans have all gone white, and the snowline will continue its descent until the first real storm arrives, since the real cold days will come and go—mostly come—along with longer nights and a deepening silence, since the winds of spring will eventually begin to stir again, the cranes will reappear, and we will notice the big wheel of life turning (even though it's turning all the time as the constellations remind us), and the sequence of events herein described will likely happen again—one might imagine time as a circular phenomenon, although it might also be that this is just a label which helps us make sense of things, that time is really just a shapeless medium through which everything moves. But speculations about the nature of time are best left to those who really understand such things; what I will say, what I can say for sure, is that I will join with those whose calendar looks more like a circle than a line, and I will pledge my allegiance to the big wheel of life which, among other things, brings the western tanagers back to the pinyon beyond this window right about now, and which offers some hope, even in this precarious era, that what has been will be again.

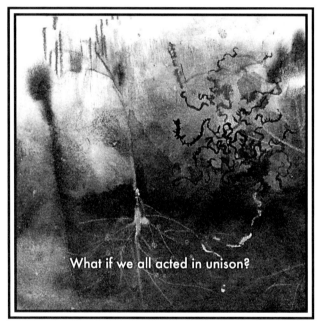

© 2022 by Andie Thrams

Loon Light

Susan McMillan

Does he know he trails long ribbons of gold over the lake's dark face?
On water smooth as obsidian, long after we watched the moon

torch fire to shaggy arrowhead tips of ancient tamarack trees
then inch itself up to steal light from stars in midnight's sky,

we sit here silent, barely breathe, our canoe adrift
like a stick on rambling current in idle autumn breeze

while close, close he passes. No color nor silhouette
gives him away as he glides dark shadows of tree-stubbled isles.

Two dazzling lines of light unwind in his fluid wake
as, with one long warbled call, he queries the soundless night.

His haunting song reverberates from shore to stony shore—
a mournful solo unreturned on this secluded lake.

Bewitched, we watch till watery distance douses his trail of flame,
then, with arms like lead reluctant, bend paddles toward sleep.

Contributors' Notes

Eric Aldrich has encountered every indigenous mammal in southern Arizona except a jaguar and a Mexican wolf. He keeps a pet black widow spider and feeds hummingbirds by hand. Eric explores urban arroyos as thoroughly as backcountry trails. Find his writing in *Terrain.org, Essay Daily*, and through his website, *ericaldrich.net*.

Dick Anderson is a husband, father, and grandfather. The Creative Consultant for the *Psychotherapy Networker,* Dick loves songwriting, photography, the Boundary Waters, Alaska, the Eastern Shore, oyster stew, walking the wild country, and his extremely loving, supportive, and talented family. For more, take a look at *www.solobydickanderson.com*.

Peter Anderson's most recent project, *Reading Colorado: A Literary Road Guide* (Bower House, September 2022), is a high-octane ride through the literature of the Centennial State. He lives on the western edge of the Sangre de Cristos where he organizes the annual Crestone Poetry Festival (poemfest.com). Visit him at *www.petehowardanderson.com*.

Marc Beaudin, a former Absaroka-Beartooth Wilderness Foundation artist-in-residence, is a poet, theatre artist, and bookseller in Livingston, Montana, with work widely anthologized in publications dedicated to environmental and social justice. A CD, *From Coltrane to Coal Train: An Eco-Jazz Suite,* featuring music by members of the band Morphine, is available at *CrowVoice.com*.

Jill Burkey's appreciation for the wild began on the ranch she grew up on in western Nebraska. She and her husband now split their time between Grand Junction and Grand Lake, Colorado, where Jill's great-grandmother opened a lodge in the '30s. Find her writing and more at *www.jillburkey.com*.

Lorraine Hanlon Comanor, former U.S. figure skating champion and U.S. team member, is a graduate of Harvard University, Stanford University School of Medicine, and Bennington Writing Seminars. A board-certified anesthesiologist, she is author/co-author of 35 medical publications and numerous personal essays. She's also an avid hiker, cross country skier, and kayaker.

Grant Deam has worked as an umpire, announcer, mower, editor, lifeguard, painter, journalist, basketball coach, Spanish teacher, bartender, writing instructor, roofer, and tutoring lab supervisor. He volunteers at St. Andrews State Park in Florida, where he lives with his wife. *grantdeam.wixsite.com/grantdeam*.

Stephanie Eardley lives on a ranch in southwest Wyoming and can most often be found along a game trail with her kids and a backpack full of books. Her work has appeared in *The Drake, Bugle Magazine*, and other publications.

Charles Finn is the author of *Wild Delicate Seconds: 29 Wildlife Encounters* and *On a Benediction of Wind: Poems and Photographs*, a pairing of his nature poetry with photographer Barbara Michelman's photos from the Pacific Northwest. He lives in Havre, Montana, with his wife Joyce Mphande-Finn and their cat Lutsa.

Gail Folkins often writes about her deep roots in the American West. She is the author of nature memoir *Light in the Trees* and nonfiction book *Texas Dance Halls: A Two-Step Circuit*. Folkins teaches at Hugo House in Seattle and is a forest steward for the Green Snoqualmie Partnership.

Diane Gansauer's trail name is "Grace," which reminds her to be more gracious to people. Grace is an interfaith minister and life-cycle celebrant who writes and presents story-enriched ceremonies, especially for the end of life. In her senior years, she has been section-hiking the Continental Divide Trail, Mexico to Canada.

Dr. Steve Gardiner was a high school English teacher for thirty-eight years in Wyoming, Peru, and Montana. He was the 2008 Montana Teacher of the Year. He has climbed mountains on five continents, including reaching 25,500 feet elevation on the North Ridge of Mount Everest.

Michael Garrigan writes and teaches along the Susquehanna River in Pennsylvania. He is the author of the poetry collection *Robbing the Pillars* and was an Artist in Residence for The Bob Marshall Wilderness Area in 2021. You can read more of his writing at *www.mgarrigan.com*.

Laura Girardeau grew up in the city limits of Eugene, Oregon, where she jumped the fence to transcribe stories the trees told her. Laura holds a master's in Environmental Studies. She enjoys hiking and writing untamable pieces at dawn, while still half-dreaming. Her work has been published in several anthologies.

Nicole Grace is a spiritual teacher and author of four books, which have won multiple international awards. She loves to visit the cathedral of wild nature and is grateful to live close enough to the Pacific Ocean to hear it roar under a full moon.

Frank Haberle's novel-in-stories, *Shufflers*, about minimum wage transients during the Reagan era, is now available from Flexible Press, and his novella, *The Biggest Slide in the World*, is with House of Hash Press. More about Frank's writing can be found on his website *www.frankhaberle.com.*

Brandon Hansen is from a village in Wisconsin's Northwoods. He spent his childhood lounging on the shores of spring-fed lakes and kept mosquitoes for company. He moved to Michigan's Upper Peninsula and spent his early 20s gawking at Lake Superior, the waters of which slosh around in his heart.

Marybeth Holleman's newest book is *tender gravity*. Others include *The Heart of the Sound* and *Among Wolves*. Raised in North Carolina's Smokies, she transplanted to Alaska's Chugach after falling for Prince William Sound two years before the Exxon Valdez oil spill. She's happiest in places where humans are outnumbered. *www.marybethholleman.com.*

Chris Kalman is an award-winning author, an editor for the *American Alpine Journal*, and a Creative Writing MFA candidate at Northern Arizona University, where he lives and climbs as much as possible. His work has been translated into Korean, and soon to be French. To learn more, visit *chriskalman.com.*

Tjibbe Kampstra enjoys hiking, camping, and photography in remote places, preferably in extreme temperatures. He has lived in the Netherlands, United States, China, France, and Mongolia. Despite having left Mongolia, Tjibbe travels back regularly to undertake adventures, most recently hiking across a frozen Khuvsgul Lake.

Talley V. Kayser teaches college courses that combine literary study with outdoor expeditions, which means she can no longer claim to be a climbing bum. But she still spends most of her summers in close contact with, and perhaps even worship of, rocks. Read more at *www.talleyvkayser.com*.

Heather Kern lives in the woods on Snoqualmie Pass, Washington with her husband and two young children. She loves to be outside, whether hiking, skiing, biking, or inspecting frogs with her kids. In nature, she feels connected and whole.

Andrea Lani is the author of *Uphill Both Ways: Hiking toward Happiness on the Colorado Trail* (Bison Books, 2022). Andrea grew up in Colorado and lives in Maine with her family. She's a Maine Master Naturalist and an editor at *Literary Mama*. Find her online at *www.andrealani.com*.

Eric le Fatte was educated at MIT and Northeastern University in biology and English. He has worked correcting catalog cards in Texas and as the Returns King at Eastern Mountain Sports, but currently hikes, writes, teaches, and does research on tiny things in the Portland, Oregon area.

Matthew Lovegrove lives in the traditional, unceded territory of the Sḵwx̱wú7mesh Nation, where he works as a curator in a small-town museum. He loves spending quality time in the Coast Mountains, exploring high alpine lakes and scrambling summits off the beaten path.

Karina Lutz worked as a sustainable energy advocate for three decades; as an editor, reporter, and magazine publisher; and making food, clothing, and shelter. She teaches yoga, sustainability, deep ecology, and writing. Her poetry books, *Preliminary Visions* and *Post-Catholic Midrashim*, can be found through *karinalutz.wordpress.com*.

Paula MacKay is a freelance writer, conservationist, and field biologist, who has studied wild carnivores for two decades. Paula earned an MFA in writing from Pacific Lutheran University. Her nature-inspired work has been published in books and anthologies, magazines, and journals. She lives in the forest near Seattle. Visit *paulamackay.com*.

Susan Marsh's writing revolves around her love for the wild world and the infinite variety of life with which we share this planet. She writes poetry, creative non-fiction, novels, and non-fiction books with a natural history theme. *Mountain Journal* publishes her occasional column, "Back to Nature."

Maeve McKenna lives with her family among forests and close to the Atlantic Ocean in rural Sligo, Ireland. Her work has been published widely and placed in several competitions. Only the trees know her secrets. Poetry holds the answers while Maeve discovers the questions. The trees know the rest.

Susan McMillan canoes, hikes, snowshoes, and cross-country skis. Her favorite place is at the end of a maple-lined portage between two lakes near the Boundary Waters. Nature is the primary inspiration for her poetry. She currently serves as poet laureate for the city of Rochester, Minnesota.

Chris Norment has spent much of the last 56 years exploring the deserts and mountains of the Western United States. He is an Emeritus Professor of Environmental Science and Ecology at the SUNY-Brockport and has published four books of creative nonfiction, most recently *Relicts of a Beautiful Sea.*

Steve Oberlechner's previous work has appeared in *The Gettysburg Review, Prairie Schooner, Cimarron Review,* and *Kestrel.* He lives with his wife and daughter in Keyser, West Virginia, and has enjoyed section-hiking the entirety of the Appalachian Trail and completing end-to-end hikes of Vermont's Long Trail and West Virginia's Allegheny Trail.

Jay Paine is a poet working on his undergraduate degree at Utah State University. When he's not writing, you can find him exploring Logan Canyon, where he enjoys his favorite nocturnal activities of night hiking and stargazing. Jay is published in *Fractured Poetics: A Poetry Anthology, The Roadrunner Review,* and *JUMP+.*

Dian Parker has traveled extensively, sleeping in shepherd huts in Sinai and in the Valley of the Dead in Palmyra before ISIS bombed the ancient city, and living in the caves of Petra with Bedouins before they were forced into housing developments. She now lives in the hills of Vermont, surrounded by forests, wildlife, and bird song. *www.dianparker.com.*

George Perreault lives in the rain shadow of the eastern Sierra Nevada and finds solace in whatever wilderness he can still find. His most recent book, *Bodark County*, is a collection of poems in the voices of characters living on the Llano Estacado in rural Texas.

Margaret Pettis has been a mule-packer, wilderness ranger, kayaker, and hiker of the Sierras, Sawtooths, High Uintas, and the Great Basin. A longtime Utah teacher and wilderness activist, she cherishes solitude. Discover her *Back Roads of Utah*, novels, and poetry at *margaretpettis. com*.

David Pratt lived for a few years in Northern Ontario, where the temperature dropped to minus 54, and he hunted moose, deer, and grouse. He now has a place on a lake in Southern Ontario, where he canoes and watches beaver and loons.

Ian Ramsey is a poet, outdoor educator, and outdoor athlete based in Maine. He directs the Kauffmann Program for Environmental Writing and Wilderness Exploration and frequently collaborates with ecologists and climate change scientists to articulate their research to non-scientists. To learn more, go to *www.ianramsey.net*.

Artist and writer **Emmy Savage** lived in south-central Colorado between 2011 and 2020. While there, she wrote about spiritual growth through attention to the natural world and how hiking in wilderness became a practice in faith. She now lives in Chicago with her family.

Sarah Scruggs learned to love the outdoors on the East Coast. She developed her own sense of adventure throughout the western part of the United States and is currently trying out life as a desert dweller. She advocates for environmental justice and outdoor inclusion whenever and wherever she is able.

Bret Serbin is a journalist in northwest Montana. She graduated from Swarthmore College with a degree in English. She's originally from Pittsburgh, Pennsylvania.

Bill Simmons, a San Joaquin Valley poet living in Carroll, Iowa, has a deep appreciation for God's creation, especially birds, which often appear in his poems. He has passed this passion on to his daughter, Rachel Clark, who is an avid and well-known birder.

David Staudt has been publishing poems, stories, and essays in literary magazines and anthologies for over forty years. His book of poems is *The Gifts and Thefts* (Backwaters Press). He has poetry forthcoming in *Epoch*. He works for the United States Equal Employment Opportunity Commission in Baltimore.

Edmond Stevens has written extensively for television and film, with his novella, "Skating to New York," adapted to film. In 2018, he received his MFA in Creative Writing from Antioch University. He attempts remote peaks, less focused on the summit than the internal journey accompanying the pursuit of wild places.

Cadence Summers inherited a deep appreciation from her parents and from a young age has enjoyed taking a long and slow wander through environments near and far, observing the small and sometimes unnoticed. She currently lives in Salt Lake City and organizes the Magic Hour Poetry Club in her community.

A passion for art and creativity led **Bessann Swanson**, the cover artist for *Deep Wild 2022*, to venture into watercolor painting in midlife. Active in the Utah watercolor community, she has exhibited widely in her home state. She has taught courses in travel sketching and takes her sketchbook on every wilderness adventure.

Wally Swist's books include *Huang Po and the Dimensions of Love* (Southern Illinois University Press, 2012), *A Bird Who Seems to Know Me: Poetry Regarding Birds and Nature* (Ex Ophidia Press, 2019), *Awakening and Visitation* (2020), *Evanescence: Selected Poems* (2020), and *Taking Residence* (2021), all with Shanti Arts.

The trailhead for the nine-mile round trip hike to the alpine Lake Melakwa is an hour from Seattle, Washington, where poet **Mary Ellen Talley** resides. She has been married to and hiked/backpacked with the young man in the poem for 52 years.

Sierra Nevada-based artist **Andie Thrams** uses watercolors in wildland forests to create paintings and artist's books exploring mystery, reverence, and delight, while grappling with the vanishing habitats of our era. Her work weaves intricate detail with hand-lettered text to evoke the complexity of ecosystems in the Greater West.

Leath Tonino is the author of two essay collections about the outdoors: *The Animal One Thousand Miles Long* and *The West Will Swallow You*. At the age of sixteen, with no prior backpacking experience, he through-hiked the Long Trail in his home state of Vermont.

Nicholas Trandahl is a United States Army veteran, poet, newspaper journalist, and outdoorsman. He lives in Wyoming with his wife and three daughters. He was the recipient of the 2019 Wyoming Writers Milestone Award and was nominated for a 2021 Pushcart Prize. He has had three collections of poetry published.

Chelsey Waters, Second Place Winner in our Graduate Student Essay Contest, is a former whitewater rafting guide and occasional flyfisherwoman. She lives in Walla Walla, Washington and studies environmental writing at Eastern Oregon University. She and her family leave in August for a year-long trip, visiting national parks and other wild places in the United States and abroad.

Kelsey Wellington, the First Place Winner in our Graduate Student Essay Contest, fell in love with the wild as a wildlife biologist, rock climber, and trail runner. Today, she works as a wildlife guide in Grand Teton and Yellowstone national parks and spends her free time deep in the backcountry, immersing herself among the peaks that inspire her writing.

About the Artists

Bessann Swanson, Cover Artist
"Halls Creek Cottonwood" and "Canyoneer"
Watercolor on paper
Utah Canyonlands

Artist's Statement: "Ever since my first summer job in Yellowstone, the wild lands of the western U.S. have captured my heart. Moving beyond iconic "calendar" scenes, I am drawn to a more intimate relationship with nature's wonders, from redrock to autumn leaves. With watercolor I try to express and share that incredible light and beauty."

A passion for art and creativity led Bessann Swanson to venture into watercolor painting in midlife. Active in the Utah watercolor community, she has exhibited widely in her home state. She has taught courses in travel sketching and takes her sketchbook on every wilderness adventure. *www.bessannswansonart.com.*

Andie Thrams, Portfolio Artist
Whiskey Tango Foxtrot
Hectograph, ink, watercolor, gouache, and tree resin on kozo.

Artist's Statement: "This series portrays forest creatures situated in strange dark places, and explores the destabilizing and dark feelings that arise with awareness of catastrophic wildfire, worldwide species extinction, habitat loss, and climate change. The images are part of the artist's book, *Whiskey Tango Foxtrot*, aka, "WTF?", an oft-heard response to environmental news. The book evokes disorientation, with no obvious way to unfold or view it, and asks questions about Earth's future. As we grapple with planetary change, it is empowering to voice difficult questions and embrace all emotions. *Whiskey Tango Foxtrot* is one of twelve artist's books included in the collaboration project, "HOPE?"

Sierra Nevada-based artist Andie Thrams uses watercolors in wildland forests to create paintings and artist's books exploring mystery, reverence, and delight, while grappling with vanishing habitats of our era. Her work weaves intricate detail with hand-lettered text to evoke the complexity of ecosystems in the Greater West. *www.andiethrams.com.*

Credits

The following work has been previously published and is reprinted here by permission of the authors:

- "The Wheel," by **Peter Anderson**, in *Colorado Central Magazine*, June 2021.
- "No Comment" and "25 Bears," by **Marc Beaudin**, in *Life List: Poems*. Riverfeet Press, 2020.
- "Summit Storm," by **Steve Gardiner**, in *Mountain Dreams: The Drive to Explore, Experience, and Expand*. Quiet Water Publishing, 2021.
- "Not the Moon," by **Marybeth Holleman**, in *tender gravity*. Red Hen Press, 2022.
- "Five Hundred Miles," by **Andrea Lani**, appears in a different form in *Uphill Both Ways: Hiking toward Happiness on the Colorado Trail*. University of Nebraska Press, 2022. Used by permission. It was originally published in *Mothers Always Write*, March 2017.
- "Secret Season," by **Maeve McKenna**, in *Channel Magazine*, Issue 4, April 2021.
- "Loon Light," by **Susan McMillan**, in *The Moccasin*, League of Minnesota Poets, 2019.
- "Our One and Only," by **Dian Parker**, in *Kingdom in the Wild*, March 5, 2019 (under the title, "You're Not the Only One".)
- "The North Fork, 2017," by **Emmy Savage**, in the *Crestone Eagle*, September 2018 (under the title, "The Rio Alto-San Isabel Trail up the North Fork"), and in *Walking the Stations in the Sangre de Cristo Mountains*, Mountain Bluebird Press, 2022.
- Portions of the work, *Whiskey Tango Foxtrot*, by **Andie Thrams**, have been published in 2022 as part of the collaboration project, HOPE? and also in the book entitled, *About HOPE?* (Both by Susan Lowdermilk, Donna Thomas, Peter Thomas, and Andie Thrams.)

Up on Mt. Garfield near Palisades, Colorado, Photo by Rick Kempa

Thank you...

for joining us on these wilderness forays in this fourth issue of *Deep Wild: Writing from the Backcountry*. Our mission is to publish the best work we can find in celebration of, and in defense of, places where there are no roads.

We are a not-for-profit journal published annually in the summer, funded by subscriptions and donations. Subscriptions are $20 for one year, $35 for two, and $45 for three, postage-paid anywhere in the United States. (Contact us for international postage rates.) Back issues are also available at reduced prices. Visit *deepwildjournal.com/subscribe*.

Submissions are open in the fall for the following year's issue. We welcome the opportunity to consider poems, stories, essays, book reviews, and art that are true to our mission. See *deepwildjournal.com/submissions* for full guidelines and exact deadlines.

To stay in touch, follow us on Facebook, Twitter, or Instagram, or on our blog at *deepwildjournal.com/blog*.

Happy hiking, climbing, kayaking, skiing, rafting, snowshoeing, canoeing...*living!*